THE SPIRIT, THE BIBLE, & WOMEN
TEACHING & STUDY GUIDE

for

In the Spirit We're Equal:
The Spirit, The Bible, & Women,
A Revival Perspective

Susan C. Hyatt

REVIVAL & RENEWAL RESOURCES
by
HYATT
PRESS
Publishing Arm of Hyatt Int'l Ministries

Dallas, Texas
2000

The Spirit, The Bible, and Women: Teaching & Study Guide for
In the Spirit We're Equal: The Spirit, The Bible, and Women—A Revival Perspective.
ISBN 1-888435-08-9
Copyright © 1999 by Hyatt International Ministries, Inc.

Published by Hyatt Press
Mailing Address (2004):
3732 Trinity Hills Lane, Euless (Fort Worth), TX 76040
Hyatt Press is a subsidiary of Hyatt International Ministries, Inc.

Phone: Metro (817) 540-9564
Email: icwhp@aol.com or info@BiblicalEquality.org
Websites: www.icwhp.org or www.BiblicalEquality.org
or www.reformationandrevival.org

Cover and book design by Susan C. Hyatt

ISBN 1-888435-11-9
Printed in the United States of America

Library of Congress
Catalog Card Number: Pending

THE SPIRIT, THE BIBLE, & WOMEN
Teaching & Study Guide
for
In the Spirit We're Equal

ABOUT THE AUTHOR

Dr. Susan C. Hyatt (b. 1946) is a church research historian, Bible scholar, ordained minister (1983) and life-long, professional educator. She graduated *with honors* from the University of New Brunswick Teachers College (1966) and Christ for the Nations Institute (1976), and *summa cum laude* from Southwestern Assemblies of God University (1987). She earned two M.A.s *with honors* from the Oral Roberts University Graduate School of Theology and Missions, one in Historical/Theological Studies with emphasis in Pentecostal/Charismatic Studies (1989); the other, in Biblical Studies (1994). She did a year of post-graduate studies at the Center for Advanced Theological Studies at Fuller Theological Seminary (1994-95) and has an earned Doctor of Ministry degree from the School of Divinity at Regent University (2000). Dr. Hyatt is the recipient of many academic awards, such as WHO'S WHO Among Students, the National Religion and Philosophy Award, National Dean's Honor's List, Academic All American, *Delta Epsilon Chi* (Honor Society of the American Association of Bible Colleges), and the Canadian Governor-General's Medal for Academic Excellence.

For almost 20 years, Susan has ghost-written for ministers who have a global impact. However, she is increasingly focusing on publishing her own material, targeting the revival-oriented, global audience. Some of her works include: *Where Are My Susannas?, 10 Things Jesus Taught about Women, Who's the Boss?, In the Spirit We're Equal, The Nature of Biblical Unity, Thinking Biblically,* and *The Spirit, The Bible, and Women.* Her doctoral dissertation: *A Biblical Theology of Womanhood for Spirit-Oriented Believers* is available at her websites: www.icwhp.org and www.biblicalequality.org. She was commissioned by Thomas Nelson Publishers to write the chapter "Spirit-Filled Women" in their benchmark publication, *The Century of the Holy Spirit,* edited by Dr. Vinson Synan. At the invitation of the French Community of the Belgium Government, she represented Pentecostal-Charismatic Women in America at the *Women in Religion Colloquium* in Brussels (2001).

Susan is the founding coordinator of the Int'l Christian Women's History Project which exists to promote biblical womanhood and to write God's women back into history. She is the founding coordinator of www.BiblicalEqualityRadio.com and of www.BiblicalEqualityInstitute.com. She is also the founding senior editor of *Biblical Equality Magazine.*

Susan and her husband, Dr. Eddie L. Hyatt, are equal partners in ministry and in marriage. Together they have planted churches, founded and directed Bible schools, and ministered internationally. They are co-founders of Hyatt Int'l Ministries and Hyatt Press. Their passion is to see genuine, Biblical Christianity prevail over fallen culture and human-centered religion. Within it, they believe, is everything that enables believers to flourish in every aspect of life,

Eddie and Susan are available to minister and to teach this course and other courses.
Or if you would like The Spirit, The Bible and Women Seminar in your area, contact:
Eddie & Susan Hyatt
3732 Trinity Hills Lane
Euless (Fort Worth), TX 76040
Email: icwhp@aol.com or Sue@BiblicalEquality.org or EddieHyatt@aol.com
Websites: www.revivalandreformation.org and www.icwhp.org and www.BiblicalEquality.org.

CONTENTS

FOREWORD

The Church has experienced unprecedented revival in the 20th century. The Pentecostal/Charismatic movement, which began in very humble surroundings at the beginning of the century, now numbers almost 600 million adherents and is growing at the rate of 23 million per year. During the final decade of the 20th century, a resurgence of revival was felt around the world, impacting many individuals, churches and denominations. But now, at the beginning of the 21st century, the revival is showing signs of fatigue, confusion and bewilderment. Many are asking, "Where do we go from here?"

For this outpouring of the Holy Spirit to continue and expand, we must have, not only revival, but also reformation. Revival can only go so far without reformation. Revival ignites and renews our love and passion for Jesus Christ and His kingdom. Reformation reforms and reshapes the doctrines and structures within which we work and serve the Lord. Whereas revival affects our feelings, reformation affects our thinking. We have had revival, but we must now have reformation. The way we think about God, church, ministry and leadership must be reshaped and reformed to come into alignment with His Word and Spirit. Only then will the Holy Spirit be able to accomplish the fullness of His plans and purposes in and through us, His people.

This present manual, along with the companion textbook, is a powerful tool for both revival and reformation. Its truth will fan into flame the gifts of God that are lying dormant throughout the Church. If allowed, it will also reform and reshape the way we think about women and the Church. As our thinking is more closely aligned with biblical truth, this will make way for, perhaps, the greatest outpouring of the Holy Spirit the Church has yet seen.

Eddie L. Hyatt, D.Min., M.Div., M.A.
Director
Revival Research Institute
Dallas, Texas
April 2000

PREFACE

The Christian belief system must be constructed on the foundation of Jesus' teaching and the Bible, accurately interpreted and confirmed by the activity of the Holy Spirit in history. This is important because the practical implications of how people think theologically about womanhood affect everything from the fulfillment of the Great Commission to the issue of self-worth to a myriad of topics in-between. Clearly, the Church needs a way of thinking about womanhood that will result in biblical behavior by women and toward women in all venues of Christian living. This course offers such an option.

This course offers men and women an opportunity to renew their minds according to the revealed will of God about half of the Body of Christ—the female members. Traditionally we have not done this, yet the Spirit moving in our day to bring our thoughts in agreement with the will of God in many areas, including how we think about womanhood.

This is important for many reason, not the least of which is the fact that, as we mature in Him, we are to think more like Him, and He taught that women are created equal with men in terms of substance and value, function and authority, privilege and responsibility. Are we able to rise to this level?

It is also important because that we renew our minds regarding womanhood because He commanded us to "go into all the world"—to men and to women of all tribes and nations— "teaching them to obey ALL" that He commanded. If we are not teaching His truth about womanhood, are we truly obeying the Great Commission?

As important as this is, however, we have a more important calling, and that is to know Him. Our ONLY CALLING is to know HIM. As we abide in Him, He gives us assignments; He asks us to do specific things for Him. We get to work with God! And this is exciting! But these assignments are only causes and must never displace the call. The cause is not the call. No matter no matter how thrilling, no matter how legitimate—the cause is not the call.

One of the assignments God has called me to—much to my surprise—is to work with Him to reform the way we think about womanhood.

Some would say, "It is a losing cause. Don't get involved!"

I am glad Martin Luther, when nudged by God his assignment to bring reform to the Church, did not think that way! I'm glad he realized God wanted the Scriptures in the hands of His people. I'm glad he realized we are saved by grace through faith alone! No, it is never a losing cause when it is God's cause executed in His time, in His way, and by His power. Biblical womanhood is such a cause—on time, on target, and only possible by His power.

And today, God is wanting to answer the prayers of His people who are crying out for more—for more of Him, for more Revival, for more souls, for more! His answer is first of all coming to us in the opportunity to reform our thinking about womanhood. He is asking us to come into agreement with His way of thinking about womanhood. If we embrace it, we become deeper and wider channels for The River to flow deeper and wider into all the earth. Won't we take the limits off God in our lives and in the Church?

Jesus Christ is building His Church and the gates of hell shall not prevail. We shall prevail in Him! Let we who profess to be His be found building—not against Him, but with Him!

ACKNOWLEDGMENTS

Many different people in many different places contributed to my life in many different ways as I prepared this course. It finally came into being as the project aspect of my doctoral dissertation. I want to thank you all, and I want you to know that it is already bringing tremendous change in the lives of men and women in the nations of the world. Thank you for your prayers and financial support that made it all possible!

I am grateful to those who gave so generously to the cost of printing this manual. Special partners in this were www.godswordtowomen.org friends Barbara Collins, Gay Anderson, and especially Pat Joyce who gave largely in memory of her mother.

As a 1976 graduate of Christ for the Nations Institute, Dallas, Texas, I was happy to have the opportunity to "come home" to share this teaching for the first time. The administration blessed me in the development of my project, graciously allowing me to proceed with full freedom in my endeavors. Thank you, C.F.N.I.

I also want to thank the C.F.N.I. students who participated in the project. Their giving of their time in the midst of an already busy schedule and their teachable spirits made the project a great success. Their responses stirred my deep and persistent sense that God wants to use this compilation of biblical and historical data to unlock life-transforming benefits for Pentecostal/Charismatic men and women all over the world, just as He did for them. Thank you, friends! Your investment is indeed reaping benefits in lives around the world!

I am also grateful to Christians for Biblical Equality. These scholars and diligent brothers and sisters have been the leading force in uncovering and promoting the message of biblical equality among Bible-believing Christians of all denominations. Who, but God Himself, can really know the full impact of their unswerving commitment to the Lordship of Jesus Christ and His Word? Thank you, my special friends, for your obedience, your love, and your sacrifice. I want to honor Dr. Catherine Clark Kroeger, the founder and President Emeritus of Christians for Biblical Equality, for giving her life without reservation to know Christ and to make Him known. And thank you, Cathie, in your very busy schedule, for giving so much into my life and, now, for serving on my doctoral committee as I prepared this manual.

I am grateful, as well, to Regent University School of Divinity for affording me the opportunity to grow in the Lord through the splendid Doctor of Ministry program. Dr. Russell West's gifted leadership of this program surpasses anything I have seen in my years as both an educator and a student. It is also an honor to have Dr. West and Dr. Mara Crabtree, Director of Women's Studies at Regent University, on my doctoral committee.

How can I adequately thank my husband, Dr. Eddie L. Hyatt? God has blessed us so much in our 24 years of marriage and ministry together. No one could have a better partner than Eddie is to me. Thank you, Eddie! Thank you for just loving and serving Jesus with your whole heart. Thank you for partnering with me in teaching my doctoral study group. We were, without trying, able to model for the participants the egalitarian marriage and ministry team that God has allowed us to be. And after all these years, He arranged that we should do it at Christ for the Nations where we met and married. God is good!

COURSE SYLLABUS
THE SPIRIT, THE BIBLE AND WOMEN

By Susan C. Hyatt, D.Min., M.A., M.A.

COURSE DESCRIPTION

This course addresses the question: What do 600-million-and-growing Pentecostal-Charismatics need to know today about biblical womanhood? This question arises in the context of the twentieth-century Pentecostal/Charismatic Revival in which a biblically sound, historically informed, Spirit-sensitive theology of womanhood is needed to counter the Church's traditional theology of womanhood and its hybrids. Whereas the traditional hierarchical model of the Church has a record of oppressing women, a Pentecostal/Charismatic model should be egalitarian model. This states that women are equal with men in terms of substance and value, function and authority, privilege and responsibility. The starting point for such a theology is the message of Jesus as revealed by word and deed in the gospel record. This harmonizes with the revealed will of God in the biblical record, particularly in the writings of Paul and in Genesis, accurately interpreted in terms of authorial intent. This theology is also in harmony with the activity of the Holy Spirit, particularly in revival history as observed in movements such as the early Friends (1650-90), the early Methodists (1739-1760), nineteenth-century revival movements in America, and the early Pentecostal/Charismatic Revival (1901- c.a. 1907).

The course consists of a 10-lesson teaching manual interfacing with the text book, In the Spirit We're Equal: The Spirit, The Bible, and Women— A Revival Perspective (ISBN 1-888435-08-9). The project's two-fold purpose is to inform and affirm. The material was tested through teaching a study group consisting of volunteers at Christ for the Nations Institute, Dallas, Texas. As a result of the course, the participants indicated a definite theological shift in favor of the egalitarian model presented. They testified to immediate changes in attitude and life-style that reflected increased harmony with biblical values.

COURSE OBJECTIVES

- To provide an atmosphere in which the Holy Spirit can teach, liberate, and heal men and women who have suffered through the erroneous precepts and practices of the Church's traditional teaching on womanhood.

- To affirm men and women who already accept the reality of biblical equality for women.

- To present biblically accurate information on the subject of biblical womanhood.

- To present historically accurate information on the subject of biblical womanhood.

- To provide the student with a biblically sound, historically informed, Spirit-oriented theology of biblical womanhood.

TEXTBOOKS AND STUDY AIDS

Hyatt, Susan C. In the Spirit We're Equal: The Spirit, The Bible, and Women—
A Revival Perspective. Dallas: Hyatt Press, 1998. (ISBN 1-888435-08-9).

Hyatt, Susan C. The Spirit, The Bible, and Women: Teaching and Study Guide. Dallas:
Hyatt Press, 2000. (ISBN 1-888435-11-9).

COURSE REQUIREMENTS

- Read In the Spirit We're Equal.

- Attend all lectures. Students should arrange their schedules so as not to miss any lectures. Should an absence occur, it is vital that the student arrange to have the session taped so that a "hole" will not occur in the student's understanding of the subject. It is important to get the whole picture regarding this topic.

- Write a 10-page paper on the material. This is done 1 page at a time following each lecture. Instructions for this reflection and interaction are given in the Application and Enrichment section of each lesson.

- Successfully complete the final examination. This is drawn directly from the Study and Review section of each lesson and is intended to reinforce the student's grasp of the material.

CLASSROOM METHODOLOGY

The primary method in this course will be classroom lectures. Additional resource material will also be provided when available. Limited use of historical, documentary video tapes may be included. When time permits, role playing of some of the leading characters may be possible. Students' participation is encouraged through questions and class discussions, but with the knowledge that most questions will be premature until the whole picture (i.e., the entire course) has been taught. Questions are best answered within the appropriate context. It is also anticipated that God will, by His grace and faithfulness, minister by His Holy Spirit in, to, and through the teachers and students.

EVALUATION PROCEDURE

Course evaluation is on the following basis:
1. Classroom participation   10%
2. Written 10-page report   40%
3. Final Exam   50%

COURSE OUTLINE

See Table of Contents.

SELECTED BIBLIOGRAPHY

Booth, Catherine. Female Ministry. Reprint of the First Ed., 1859. New York: Salvation Army Printing & Publishing Dept., 1975.

Bristow, John Temple. What Paul Really Said About Women. New York: Harper and Row, 1988. Pp. 3-5.

Brown, Judy L. Women Ministers According to Scripture. Morris Publishing, 1996.

Bushnell, Katherine. God's Word to Women. Mossville, IL: God's Word to Women Publishers, Reprint. N.d.

CBE Statement: Men, Women & Biblical Equality. http://www.cbeinternational.org or CBE, 122 W. Franklin Ave., Ste. 218, Minneapolis, MN 55404-2451. http://www.cbeinternational.org or 1 (877) 285-2256. See also the CBE Catalog.

Chilcote, John Wesley. John Wesley and the Women Preachers of Early Methodism. Metuchen: Scarecrow, 1991.

Fee, Gordon. Commentary on the First Epistle to the Corinthians. Grand Rapids: Eerdmans, 1987.

Francen, Kim. Forsaken But Not Forgotten. Tulsa: FWO Books, 1996.

Hull, Gretchen Gaebelein. Equal to Serve. Grand Rapids: Baker, 1987, 1991, 1998.

Hyatt, Eddie L. 2000 Years of Charismatic Christianity. Dallas: Hyatt Press, 1996, 1998.

Hyatt, Susan C. Where Are My Susannas? Dallas: Hyatt Press, 1997.

Kroeger, Richard Clark and Catherine Clark Kroeger. I Suffer Not a Woman: Rethinking 1 Timothy 2:11-15 in Light of Ancient Evidence. Grand Rapids: Baker, 1992.

Kroeger, Catherine Clark and James R. Beck. Women, Abuse and the Bible. Grand Rapids: Baker, 1996.

Mickelsen, Alvera and Berkeley. "Does Male Dominance Tarnish Our Translations?" Christianity Today. Oct. 5, 1979.

Penn, William. "The Preface." Vol. 1. The Works of George Fox. 8 Vols. 1706 Reprint. New York: AMS Press, 1975.

Phillips, J. B. Your God Is too Small. New York: MacMillan, 13th printing, 1972.

Raycroft, Mary Audrey. Releasers of Life. Shippensburg: Destiny Image, 1998.

Schmidt, Alvin John. Veiled and Silenced: How Culture Shaped Sexist Theology. Macon: Mercer University Press, 1989.

Study Bible for Women: The New Testament. Ed. Catherine Kroeger, Mary Evans, and Elaine Storkey. Grand Rapids: Baker Books, 1995.

Swidler, Leonard. "Jesus Was a Feminist," Catholic World. Jan. 1971.

Tucker, Ruth A. and Walter Liefeld. Daughters of the Church: Women and Ministry from New Testament Times to the Present. Grand Rapids: Zondervan, 1987.

GLOSSARY

Term	Definition
Complementarian	The idea that married couples are to fit together on the basis of gender, with the man as the dominant partner, rather than on the basis of gifts, talents, callings, anointings, or other factors.
Egalitarian	The idea that men and women are equal in substance, value, and function.
Hierarchical	The idea of an authoritative, chain-of-command pattern in relationships.
Hierarchy	An authoritative chain-of-command with authority residing at the top and that authority being delegated in descending order through subordinates.
Institutionalism	An emphasis on organization at the expense of other factors. It is a mode of organization whereby human control displaces the leadership of the Holy Spirit
Matriarchal	Adjective form of a chain-of-command in which women rule authoritatively by delegated authority.
Matriarchy	An authoritative chain-of-command pattern of relationships in which women rule with authority over men.
Metaphor	A comparison between two unlike objects that have one thing in common.
Misogynous	Adjective form for the idea of woman-hating
Misogyny	Noun form for the idea of woman-hating.
Patriarchal	The idea that men are to rule.
Patriarchy	An authoritative chain-of-command pattern of relationships in which men rule with authority over women.
World View	A perspective one takes in looking at all of life, acting somewhat like a filter through which everything is understood.

HELPFUL HINTS

This manual is specifically designed to meet certain criteria.

- **This manual is not intended to stand on its own as a teaching tool. It is designed to be used with the textbook, <u>In the Spirit We're Equal: The Spirit, The Bible, and Women—A Revival Perspective</u>. Statements in this teaching tool should not be taken out of the context in which they occur in the textbook.**

- It is designed as a guide for the teacher who is teaching this material for the first time, but it is also flexible enough to be used by the most experienced in the field of biblical womanhood and equality.

- It is also designed to help the student grasp and assimilate the material.

The material is designed for ease in lecturing and learning.

- The "Suggested Reading and Teaching Resources" provide helpful additional research material for the teacher, but even without reference to these, the course content is good entry-level material.

- The format of the "Lecture Outline" section includes a right-hand column for teacher or student questions, special notes, reminders, and the page references in the textbook.

- The "Application and Enrichment Projects" section at the end of each lesson offers opportunities for fun, reflection, and research that will suit the beginner while challenging the advanced student. These need not be done in the duration of the course but can be continued over an extended period long after the official course has ended.

- A brief "Study and Review" section affords the student another opportunity to go over the material in each lesson. The Answer Key for these questions is included after Lesson 10. Questions from the Study and Review sections form the basis of the final exam.

- A short-answer exam is included along with the answer key.

- Each student is strongly encouraged to write a one-page (250-word) essay immediately following each lesson, placing emphasis on the part(s) that was most interesting or useful to the student. The paper should be double-spaced and typed in 12-point, Times Roman font. At the completion of the course, the student will have a 10-page paper covering the material and his or her interaction with the material.

> NOTE: Although the manual is designed in a 10-lesson format,
> it is readily adaptable to time frames and number of lessons
> allotted in various educational settings.

LESSON 1

Becoming Aware of Biblical Womanhood

LESSON 1
Becoming Aware of Biblical Womanhood

- ❏ THEME: The Christian message regarding womanhood must reflect with integrity the message of Jesus as revealed in the Bible, accurately interpreted, and in Church history as revealed by the activity of the Holy Spirit, especially in times of revival.

- ❏ PURPOSE: To establish the probable need to correct the student's understanding of biblical womanhood.

- ❏ OBJECTIVES:

    1. To provide a context in which the Holy Spirit can teach each person.

    2. To raise personal awareness of some of the issues that feed into prevailing ideas about biblical womanhood.

    3. To delineate some of the reasons that we need an accurate understanding of biblical womanhood.

    3. To generate a sense of expectation of what this course can mean to each man and woman personally as well as to the Church.

- ❏ TEXTBOOK READING: Preface (pp. ix-xii) and Chapter 1 (pp. 3-10).

    Hyatt, Susan C. In the Spirit We're Equal: The Spirit, The Bible, and Women—A Revival Perspective. Dallas: Hyatt Press, 1998.

- ❏ SUGGESTED READING AND TEACHING RESOURCES:

    - Francen, Kim. Forsaken But Not Forgotten. Tulsa: Francen World Outreach. 1996. Available from Francen World Outreach, P. O. Box 701978, Tulsa, OK 74170 USA.

    - Perceptual Ambiguity Sketch of Woman, 1888, no copyright. http://www.illusionworks.com/html/perceptual_ambiguity.html.

    - Procure a large, framed, colorful painting or photograph to use as a teaching aid in Part II.C.

    - Schmidt, John Alvin. Veiled and Silenced: The Role of Culture in Shaping Sexist Theology. Macon: University of Georgia, 1989. ISBN 0-86554-327-5.

❑   LECTURE OUTLINE:

I.   ENTRANCE QUESTIONNAIRE

        A.   Instructions

                1.   Each student is to complete the questionnaire prior to any teaching.

                2.   A copy of the questionnaires goes to the teacher. A tear-out copy for
                        this purpose is included in Appendix 1.

        B.   Purpose

                1.   This questionnaire will raise each student's awareness of some of the
                        issues that feed into their theological position on biblical womanhood.

                2.   The questionnaire will also alert the teacher to the prevailing theology
                        and personal mindset of the each of the students.

Instructions: Circle the response that most closely describes your belief. A space following
each statement provides room for you to make a brief comment if this would be helpful.

1. YES. NO. I DON'T KNOW. I believe God has male gender.

2. YES. NO. I DON'T KNOW. I believe husbands are to exercise authority over their wives.

3. YES. NO. I DON'T KNOW. I believe men are to exercise authority over women in
    ministry.

4. YES. NO. I DON'T KNOW. I believe woman as "helper" (or "help meet" or "help mate")
    in Genesis means that God calls women to be subordinate helpers of men.

5. YES. NO. I DON'T KNOW. I believe the word "submit" in Paul's writings means that
    women are to come under the authority of men.

6. YES. NO. I DON'T KNOW. I believe the Bible prescribes different roles for men and
    women based solely on gender.

7. YES. NO. I DON'T KNOW. I believe women are equal in substance but subordinate in
    function and authority.

8. YES. NO. I DON'T KNOW. I believe Jesus taught chain-of-command principles in relationships.

9. YES. NO. I DON'T KNOW. I believe women can prophesy but should not judge prophecy.

10. YES. NO. I DON'T KNOW. I believe Paul taught chain-of-command principles in relationships.

11. YES. NO. I DON'T KNOW. I believe there is subordination (chain-of-command) in the Trinity.

12. YES. NO. I DON'T KNOW. I believe qualified women should be able to occupy the top positions of authority in the Church.

13. YES. NO. I DON'T KNOW. I believe women should be able to teach men as well as women.

14. YES. NO. I DON'T KNOW. I believe women need an accoountability "covering."

15. YES. NO. I DON'T KNOW. I believe women can be apostles.

16. YES. NO. I DON'T KNOW. I believe women can be prophets.

17. YES. NO. I DON'T KNOW. I believe women can be evangelists.

18. YES. NO. I DON'T KNOW. I believe women can be senior pastors.

19. YES. NO. I have studied Church history.
If so, in your opinion, how much?

20. YES. NO. I have studied women in Church history.
If so, in your opinion, how much?

II.   THE NATURE OF THE COURSE

A.   Jesus, the Only Legitimate Starting Point

B.   Personal Remarks and Motivations of the Teacher

Read Preface, pp. ix-xii.

C.   The Need to Examine the Parts of this Issue One Piece at a Time in Order to Understand the Big Picture.

Show a large painting or picture. Explain that this is like our mental picture of womanhood in that it is composed of many different parts that work together to produce the whole picture.

D.   The Nature of the Course

1.   For whom is this course intended?

a.   This course is for both men and women.

b.   This course is for Pentecostal/Charismatic and Revival-oriented believers.

In this course, we will talk about the individual parts in an orderly way. It is important for the student to focus on the part under discussion and not be distracted by another area of concern. That concern will be dealt with at an appropriate point in the course.

2.   What is this course really about?

Here is some advice!

a.   This course is not about women in ministry but about biblical womanhood because what we believe about womanhood determines what we believe women can and should experience in terms of relationships, opportunity, marriage, quality of life, self-esteem, and ministry.

Be attentive, patient, and teachable. Write down your questions. If they are not answered at some point in the course, then submit them. It is important that your questions be answered. Be willing to get the whole picture, piece by piece, and then look again at any area(s) you find difficult.

b.   This course is a journey into Biblical truth, with Jesus as the starting point.

c.   This course is unique in that it draws from both the best of current Conservative biblical studies and revival historical studies.

3.   What are some of the strategic positions maintained in this course?

    a.   This course presents an egalitarian world view because the biblical and historical evidence supports a Christian world view that is, in fact, egalitarian rather than hierarchical.

    b.   This course does not promote a "victim mentality." In Christ, women are not victims but victors, but women are victims of ignorance until they have accurate knowledge.

    c.   This course is not pro-woman/anti-man but promotes an equally high regard and respect for both, and does not promote matriarchy.

    d.   This course affirms women through accurate biblical and historical knowledge.

Define egalitarian and hierarchical. Refer to the Glossary.

What is a Christian world view?

Define patriarchy and matriarchy. Refer to the vocabulary section.

What does it mean "to be affirmed"?

III.   RATIONALE FOR THIS COURSE

A.   A Biblical Theology of Womanhood Is Essential Because the Way a Person Thinks about Womanhood Determines Behavior in Relation to Women.

B.   The Christian Belief System about Womanhood Must Reflect Biblical Truth.

1.   It must be constructed on the foundation of Jesus' teaching.

2.   It must embrace the whole Bible, accurately interpreted.

3.   It must be confirmed by the activity of the Holy Spirit in the Bible and in church history.

The Word and the Spirit agree.

C.   The Traditional Way of Thinking about
     Womanhood often Is Not Biblically Sound.

     1.   The traditional theology of
          womanhood was developed under
          the influence of pagan concepts (i.e.
          woman is evil, unclean, unequal, and
          inferior).

     2.   The traditional theology of
          womanhood gives rise to
          "convenient" doctrines that, because
          they are simply modified forms of
          the traditional theology of
          womanhood, continue to propagate
          traditional error and subjugation.

     3.   The traditional theology of
          womanhood hinders fulfillment of
          the Great Commission because the
          hierarchical message being
          propagated is at odds with the
          teachings of Jesus.

     4.   The traditional theology of
          womanhood leads to confusion and
          inner conflict resulting in unhealthy
          attitudes and actions among
          Christian women.

     5.   The traditional theology of
          womanhood produces abusive
          behavior toward women.

     6.   The traditional theology of
          womanhood serves as fodder for
          erroneous perceptions of biblical
          manhood.

     7.   The traditional theology of
          womanhood drives many women
          away from Christianity, giving rise
          to perversion, witchcraft, paganism,
          feminism, and New Age mysticism.

p. 56; 63-64; 65. For an in-depth reading, see Veiled and Silenced by Alvin John Schmidt.

For example, the so-called complementarian notion that women are equal in substance but different in function and subordinate in authority is rooted in traditional theology, not biblical principles.

The percentage of the global population professing to be Christian has remained at 34% since 1900. Is the restriction of womanhood, in disobedience to the Great Commission, a factor?

pp. 4-5

pp. 5-9

Pre- or post-lecture, scan Ch. 18, pp 275-89.

Pre- or post-lecture, scan Ch. 19, pp 291-98.

IV.   EXPECTED RESULTS

    A.   Women Will Benefit.

        1.   Believing women will experience affirmation.

        2.   Believing women will no longer feel the need to manipulate others because they will no longer be under the control of others.

        3.   Believing women will begin to function in all of life out of their biblical identity in Christ alone rather than out of cultural and religious dictates.

    B.   Women Previously Resistant to the Gospel May Listen.

        1.   A Church that is aware of and repentant of its misogynous history can become a humble, Spirit-led voice for educated women.

        2.   Women previously resistant will respond to the message of Jesus, a message that treats them as equals with men in substance and function.

        3.   Participants will encounter biblical truth about womanhood that will challenge their cultural and religious understanding.

        4.   Participants will become more aware of Church history in relation to womanhood.

    C.   Men Will Benefit.

        1.   Men will be free from obligatory leadership thrust upon them by the traditional theology of manhood and womanhood.

2.   Men will be set free of the pride, privilege, prejudice, and power-politics set in motion by the traditional theology of manhood/womanhood.

Scan pp. 291-293 to get a general sense of what is intended here.

3.   The Church will no longer, by its theology, sanction domestic abuse.

Scan pp. 59-63 to get some perspective on this.

D.   Men and Women Will Have a Biblically Sound Option.

1.   Men and women will have a biblically-accurate, historically-informed, Spirit-oriented theology of womanhood.

2.   Men and women will gain accurate meanings of helper, headship, covering, and submission and other biblical concepts that have been used to formulate the traditional theology that subjugates women.

3.   Awakened to Biblical Truth about Womanhood, men and women will have the opportunity to repent of traditional attitudes and behavior.

Jesus also said, "You shall know the truth and the truth shall set you free" (Jn. 8:32).

4.   Men and women will receive healing and deliverance, best defined by Jesus' words in Luke 4:18-19.

Jesus said, "The Spirit of the Lord is upon Me because He has anointed Me to preach the gospel to the poor. He has sent Me to heal the broken-hearted, to preach deliverance to the captives and recovery of sight to the blind, to set at liberty those who are oppressed, to preach the acceptable year of the Lord" (Lk. 4:18-19).

E.   The Church Will Benefit.

1.   Aware of its shameful past and erroneous, self-serving theology, the Church will have an opportunity to repent and become an effective voice for God in the evangelization of women.

2.   The Church will increase with a growth that is from God.

3.   Repentance will facilitate great inbreakings of the Spirit of God, that is, REVIVAL.

F.   Testimonies from Previous Students

1.   God brought to memory those times I had been blamed, shamed, and tamed, so that He could heal me through this material and the Spirit. I felt like weeping the entire time.

2.   I always felt that if I could understand what the Bible really says about women then I could stand firm in whatever God had me pursue. You have taken the limitations off my thinking and future plans!

3.   A life-changer! It set me free. It helped me understand so much. When I get married, my pre-marriage counseling must include this teaching. We desperately need this!

4.   This course was right on time. It was such a deliverance for me.

5.   I feel free at last! I no longer despise the fact that God created me female. I have been delivered from a woman-hating spirit.

6.   I am so glad you verbalized what my heart has been telling me my entire life.

7.   This course has been nothing short of a miracle for me. I feel more of God's love than ever before and a surge of faith that I never felt before.

8.   I always knew (something in me knew) that women are equal with men. I just didn't know how to prove it. Now I do!

9.   I am so excited about this course. I believe it will help bring true Revival.

10.   I want to teach this material!

V.   CONCLUSION

    A.   Traditional Christian Teaching about Womanhood Must Be Replaced by a
        Biblical Theology of Womanhood.

        1.   The Church's traditional theology of womanhood is contrary to the
            teaching of the Bible, accurately interpreted, and the activity of the
            Holy Spirit, observed in Church history.

        2.   We are to think about womanhood as Jesus taught in word and deed.

    B.   We Are to Renew Our Minds (Rm. 12:2).

        1.   Read and consider the legend of Procrustes on page 10 of the textbook.

        2.   Getting a new perspective requires a paradigm shift, or a "revelation,"
            or a simple openness to see something from a different perspective.
            Consider the optical illusion below. Do you see a young woman? An
            elderly woman? Or both?

            This anonymous illustration of perceptual ambiguity comes from an
            1888 German postcard.
            http://www.illusionworks.com/html/perceptual_ambiguity.html

APPLICATION AND ENRICHMENT PROJECTS

1.   Begin an assessment of your own life and thinking to discover if your understanding of biblical womanhood reflects the influence of traditional theology.

2.   Of the reasons given for this course, which one interests you the most?

3.   Read Kim Francen's booklet, Forsaken But Not Forgotten. Kim and Mike Francen conduct mass evangelism crusades in nations all around the world, and Kim conducts women's conferences in Asia, Africa, and America. Living with the plight of women constantly before her, Kim writes from first-hand experience of womanhood's cry for help. And she is responding by preaching the Message of Jesus.

4.   Explore web sites to get current information on the condition of womanhood in the nations. It may be necessary to go to feminist web sites since the Church, for the most part, has ignored the oppression of womanhood in the nations. Suggestions include: http://www.feminist.com and http://www.awomansvoice.com.

5.   Begin to educate yourself about the cultural norms for women in another nation and pray about how to communicate the Jesus message about women to that culture.

6.   Begin to educate yourself about women in Islam. How can they be reached with the Gospel? What is the difference between what Jesus teaches them about themselves and what the Koran teaches them? One helpful book on this issue is Women in Islam by P. Newton and M. Rafiqul Haqq. It is published by I. F. Publications and is available from I. F., P. O. Box 60518, Pasadena, CA 91106.

7.   Begin your own bibliography related to this course, and when you come across additional books related to this lesson, add them, noting why that book(s) is helpful.

8.   Begin to collect articles related to this course, and when you come across items related to this lesson, file them in your personal file.

9.   Review the lesson and do the Study and Review section on the next page.

10.   Write a one-page (250-word) essay on the material in this lesson, placing emphasis on the part(s) that were most interesting or useful to you. Your paper should be double-spaced and should be typed in 12-point, Times Roman font. This will constitute page 1 of a paper that may be considered as part of a final grade in this course.

FOR STUDY AND REVIEW

PART I

Based on the teaching in this lesson, indicate if the following statements are true or false by inserting a T or an F in the space provided.

1. ____ Jesus is the only legitimate starting point for a biblically sound theology of womanhood.

2. ____ This course is only for women.

3. ____ Men can benefit from this course.

4. ____ Students of this course will probably encounter biblical truth about womanhood that will challenge ideas they have been taught by culture and religion.

5. ____ What we believe about womanhood determines what we believe women can and should experience in terms of relationships, opportunity, marriage, quality of life, self-esteem, and ministry.

PART II

Complete the sentences by selecting the best answers from the following6:

    ** Jesus ** biblical ** evil ** historical ** inferior ** message ** activity **
       ** renew * unclean * abusive * repent * unequal ** Spirit **

1. This course draws on both _____ and _____ studies.

2. The Church's traditional way of thinking about womanhood was developed under the influence of the pagan concepts that woman is _____, _____, _____, and _____.

3. The Christian message regarding womanhood must reflect with integrity the _____ of _____ as revealed in the Bible, accurately interpreted, and in Church history as revealed by the _____ of the Holy _____, especially in times of revival.

4. It can be shown that the traditional way of thinking about womanhood has produced _____ behavior toward women.

5. Awakened to biblical truth about womanhood, perhaps for the first time, men and women will have the opportunity, if necessary, to _____ and _____ their minds.

LESSON 2

What Did Jesus and the Believers
in the New Testament Teach
about Biblical Womanhood?

LESSON 2

What Did Jesus and the Believers in the New Testament Teach about Women?

❑ THEME: Jesus lived in "a man's world," but He treated women as equal with men in terms of substance and value, function and authority, privilege and responsibility.

❑ PURPOSE: To discover what Jesus said about women through His earthly life and through His Holy Spirit in the early Church.

❑ OBJECTIVES:

    1.   To become aware of the prevailing status of women in the culture of Jesus' day.

    2.   To compare this with how Jesus related to women.

    3.   To show that the Holy Spirit continued to relate to women in the way that Jesus had.

    4.   To show that the Church of the New Testament adopted the theology of womanhood taught by Jesus in all aspects of life and ministry.

    5.   To show that Jesus demonstrated His apparent belief that women were equal with men in terms of substance and value, function and authority, privilege and responsibility.

❑ TEXTBOOK READING: Chapter 2 (pp. 13-20) and Chapter 3 (pp. 21-35)

❑ SUGGESTED READING AND TEACHING RESOURCES:

- Assemblies of God White Paper on The Role of Women in the Church. http://www.ag/whitepapers

- The Holy Bible: New Testament and Psalms. NIV Inclusive Language Edition. London: Hodder and Stoughton and the International Bible Society, 1995 edition.

- Phillips, J. B. Your God Is too Small. New York: MacMillan, 13th printing, 1972.

- Study Bible for Women: The New Testament. Ed. Catherine Kroeger, Mary Evans, and Elaine Storkey. Grand Rapids: Baker Books, 1995.

- Swidler, Leonard. "Jesus Was a Feminist," Catholic World. Jan. 1971.

❑ LECTURE OUTLINE:	QUESTIONS, NOTES, AND TEXTBOOK REFERENCES

I.   OBSERVATIONS REGARDING THE CULTURE OF JESUS' DAY

Principle: In general, we miss the gender equality expressed by the radical nature of Jesus' actions because we lack knowledge of the oppressive conditions suffered by women of that day. We can gain some insight, through listening to the hostility expressed in religious writings of the day.

A.   Evidence of Sexist Attitudes in Jesus' Day.

1.   Examples of religious beliefs and practices in Jesus' day illustrate the negative attitude toward women.

    Read from pp. 13-14.

2.   Examples of social practices in Jesus' day also help us understand the deprecation of women.

    Read from p. 14.

B.   Absence of Anti-Woman Sentiment in the Gospel Record

1.   The Gospel writers never portray a negative attitude toward women.

    pp. 14-15

2.   The Gospels never attribute a prescribed, subservient role to women that would be in keeping with the cultural role given women in that day.

3.   The Gospel writers show that Jesus countered these sexist attitudes.

II.   THE PERSPECTIVE OF JESUS: WOMEN ARE EQUAL WITH MEN.

    pp. 15-20

Principle: Jesus lived in "a man's world," but He went against the norms of patriarchal culture by treating women as persons equal with men. He countered the ideas that women were unequal, inferior, unclean, and evil. The reverse of that statement is enlightening: women are equal, not inferior, clean, and good.

A.	Jesus Demonstrates the Equal Personhood of Woman	pp. 15-16
	1. Jn. 8:3-11 – The Woman Caught in Adultery	
	2. Matthew 9:20-22. – Jesus Heals the Woman with the Issue of Blood	
B.	Jesus Shows Woman's Equality in Marriage	p. 16
	Mt. 8:1-11 - Jesus revealed important insights about his theology of womanhood in his discussion about marriage and divorce.	
C.	Jesus Shows Woman's Equal Social Status	p. 16
	Jn. 4:26, 39-42 - Jesus' Encounter with the Woman at the Well	
D.	Jesus Projects God in the Image of Woman	p. 17
	1. He compares His desire to protect and care for Jerusalem with the protective instincts of a mother hen spreading her wings over her brood (Mt. 23:37; Lk. 13:34).	Why did He not use a strong male metaphor, perhaps that of a warrior? Why did He use a female image to portray God?
	2. In the parable about the woman who found the lost coin (Lk. 15:8-10), the woman represented God.	Why did Jesus choose a female metaphor?
E.	Jesus Gives a Lesson in Biblical Equality	p. 17 According to this incident, what is the defining issue in relation to Jesus?
	Lk. 8:19-21 – Jesus Responds to a Visit from His Family	
F.	Jesus Rejects the Notion of Woman's Role.	p. 18
	Lk. 10:38-42 - Jesus Visits the Home of Martha and Mary	
G.	Jesus Rejects the Cultural Perception of Womanhood	p. 18-19
	Lk. 11:27-28 – Jesus Rebuffs a Woman Who Compliments Him.	

H.   The Risen Christ Commissions the First   pp. 19-20
     Apostle—A Woman!

     Jn. 10-10-18/Mt. 28:1-10

I.   Summary Statement of Jesus Teaching on
     Women

     Jesus was a friend of women. He vigorously
     promoted the dignity and equality of women
     in terms of substance and value, function
     and authority, privilege and responsibility,
     and He left us this example. Is it not our
     responsibility to emulate His attitudes and
     behavior?

III. THE PERSPECTIVE OF THE EARLY CHURCH: p. 21
     WOMEN WERE EQUAL WITH MEN.

     Principle: The Spirit continued to advance the idea
     of equality for women. Working in and through the
     first generation of believers, the Spirit promoted
     Jesus' teaching about women. Despite the pressures
     of a patriarchal world, the believers in Acts
     demonstrate a remarkable tendency toward that
     equality.

     A.   Equality in the Upper Room (Acts 1:13-26)   p. 21

          In keeping with Jesus' egalitarian social
          pattern, both men and women participated in
          prayer and decision-making in the Upper
          Room (Acts 1:13-26).

     B.   Equality at Pentecost (Acts 1:13-26)   pp. 21 & 23

          The Spirit confirmed Jesus' egalitarian
          pattern, when, on the Day of Pentecost,
          women were equal recipients of the
          Pentecostal outpouring (Acts 2:1-4,17-18).

     C.   Equality in Marriage   pp. 21 & 34

          1.   References: Acts 1:13-26 / Lk. 8:1-
               3; 23:49,55; 24:10; Eph. 5:21ff.

          2.   He overrides Numbers 30 and holds
               women directly responsible to God.

3.   He holds Ananias, the husband, responsible for his actions, and He holds Sapphira individually and personally responsible for her behavior (Acts 5:1-11).

D.   Equality in Redemption   p. 22

     1.   Reference: Acts 1:13-26

     2.   Women were redeemed to the same degree as men, and all ramifications belonged to both equally (Acts 5:14).

     3.   In both proclamation and practice, wherever Paul went, he clearly acknowledged gender equality in redemption (Acts 17:34, 12; 34).

E.   Equality in Daily Life   p. 22

     1.   Reference: Acts 1:13-26

     2.   Research shows that Christian women in Jerusalem exercised considerable freedom and equality in domestic and spiritual functions.

F.   Equality in Biblical Ministry   Familiarize yourself with the biblical definition of ministry on pp. 23-28.

Ministry in the New Testament is the Spirit-empowered expression of God to us and through us. It is a privilege and responsibility of all believers. It is not an office such as we have today.

     1.   Women functioned as CO-WORKERS with Paul   pp. 28-29

          a.   References: 1 Cor. 16:16 / Rom. 16:1-16 / Phil. 4:2-3.

          b.   Paul mentions women as being co-laborers or coworkers (Greek, sunergoi) with him in ministry (1 Cor. 16:16, 19; Rom. 16:1-16; Phil. 4:2-3).

c.   In Romans 16:3-16, Paul speaks of Mary (16:6), Tryphana, Tryphosa, and Persis (16:12).

a.   Two of Paul's coworkers were Euodia and Syntyche, two women who worked beside him, not under him (Phil. 4:2-3).

2.   Women functioned as PASTORS.   pp. 29-31

a.   References: Acts 12:12 / Acts 16:13-15, 40 / 1 Cor. 1:11; 16:19 / Rom.. 16:3-5 / Col. 4:15, 2 / 3 Jn.

b.   In the NT and until at least the third century, believers gathered in homes to worship.

c.   In the NT, several of the homes where believers gathered are described in terms of the woman, not the man, of the house.

d.   Was Phoebe a servant, minister, or deacon (Rom. 16:1-2)?

3.   Women functioned as TEACHERS   p. 31

a.   References: Acts 18:1-4 / Col. 3:16 / Col. 1 1:2; 3:12 / 1 Cor. 14:26, 31

b.   Priscilla was a teacher, and in Corinth, Paul shared in ministry with her and her husband Aquila (Acts 18:1-4; 18-28).

4.   Women functioned as PROPHETS   pp. 31-32

a.   References: Acts 2:17 / Acts 21:8-9 / 1 Cor. 11:4-5 / 1 Cor. 14:3-4; 26, 31

        b.   Women (e.g., Deborah, Miriam, Huldah, Anna) had functioned as prophetesses before Pentecost, but one result of the coming of the Spirit "upon all flesh" was, "Your sons and daughters will prophecy" (Acts 2:17).

     5.   Women functioned as APOSTLES.   p. 32

        a.   Reference: Rom. 16:7

        b.   Paul refers to Junia as an apostle (Rom. 16:7).

G.   Women Functioned in Business Outside the Home   p. 33

     1   References: Acts 16:14 / Acts 17:32 / Acts 18:2-3 / Rom. 16;1-2.

     2   In the NT, Christian women were not confined to domestic roles as is often suggested today as the proper biblical model for women.

     3   The New Testament mentions women who worked outside the home in commerce: Lydia (Acts 16:14), Damaris (Acts 17:32), Priscilla (Acts 18:2-3), and Phoebe (Rom. 16:1-2).

IV.   CONCLUSION

A.   Jesus Taught Equality in Word and Action.

B.   This Equality Continued to Be Demonstrated by the Holy Spirit in the Midst of the New Testament Church.

C.   We Are to Follow the Example of Jesus, Empowered by His Spirit.

D.   Is This Egalitarian Message of Jesus a Part of Our Message?

APPLICATION AND ENRICHMENT PROJECTS

1.   Do you know of any Old Testament images of God that depict God in feminine terms? Explore this through your biblical study helps.

2.   Have you considered the significance of the term "Father" in reference to God? Jesus called him "Father." Why? Consider the intimacy He was conveying. Also consider the difference between the personal God of Israel, Yaweh, and the capricious, impersonal "gods" of the heathens. Is it acceptable or necessary to limit Almighty God to the title "Father," when He is so much more? How big is God? Read the small book, Your God Is too Small, by J. B. Phillips.

3.   Had Jesus come as a woman in the Incarnation, would He have been able to penetrate a patriarchal, misogynous (woman-hating) culture?

4.   Read Leonard Swidler's paper: "Jesus Was a Feminist," Catholic World (Jan. 1971). This is available in any good theological library and through Christians for Biblical Equality at http://www.cbeinternational.org or at 1 (877) 285-2256.

5.   Purchase a copy of the NIV Inclusive Language Edition of the New Testament.

6.   Study the material on the Christians for Biblical Equality Web site regarding the NIV Inclusive Language Edition at http://www.cbeinternational.org.

7.   Continue to be alert for reference helps regarding this lesson. Add these titles to your bibliography, books to your library, and articles to your files.

8.   Review the lesson and do the Study and Review section on the next page.

10.   Write a one-page (250-word) essay on the material in this lesson, placing emphasis on the part(s) that were most interesting or useful to you. Your paper should be double-spaced and should be typed in 12-point, Times Roman font. This will constitute page 2 of a paper that may be considered part of a final grade in this course.

FOR STUDY AND REVIEW

<u>PART I</u>

Based on the teaching in this lesson, indicate if the following statements are true or false by inserting a T or an F in the space provided.

1.   ____ Jesus taught equality by what He said and what He did.

2.   ____ The story of Ananias and Sapphira illustrates that God holds husbands and wives each individually, personally, and directly responsible to Him for their behavior.

3.   ____ The believers in Acts demonstrate a remarkable tendency toward the equality Jesus taught.

4.   ____ Women were not allowed to function as apostles.

5.   ____ On occasion, Jesus projected God in the image of woman.

<u>PART II</u>

Complete the sentences by selecting the best answers from the following:

** Spirit ** marriage ** roles ** co-workers **
** ministry ** woman **

1.   Jesus demonstrated woman's equality in both _____ and _____.

2.   Jesus rejected the notion that women are to be restricted to certain _____.

3.   The Risen Christ commissioned the first apostle—a _____.

4.   Euodia and Syntyche were _____ with Paul who worked with him, not under him.

5.   The _____ continued to advance the idea of equality of men and women in terms of substance and value, function and authority, privilege and responsibility.

LESSON 3

The Critical Downward Turn
for the Church and Women

LESSON 3
The Critical Downward Turn
for the Church and Women

□ THEME: In the second century, a critical conflict between institutionalizing forces and Spirit-led believers climaxed, and this conflict would be instrumental in determining the fate of the Church and of Christian women, in particular.

□ PURPOSE: To show the strategic, historical turning point away from the message of Jesus and the plunge into the Dark Ages for the Church and women.

□ OBJECTIVES:

     1.   To identify when, where, and how the message of Jesus was lost.

     2.   To show the struggle between the Spirit-focused forces and the institutionalizing churchmen as revealed through events related to the Montanist Revival.

     3.   To spell out clearly the detrimental effects for believing women.

□ TEXTBOOK READING: Chapter 4, Pages 39-56

□ SUGGESTED READING AND TEACHING RESOURCES:

     •   Hyatt, Eddie L. Montanism: Pagan Frenzy or Pentecostal Fervor? This thoroughly researched and extensive study of the Montanists is available from the author. In abbreviated form, it appears in the Compendium of the Society for Pentecostal Studies, 26th Annual Meeting, March 13-15, 1997. EddieHyatt@aol.com

     •   Hyatt, Eddie L. "Part 3." 2000 Years of Charismatic Christianity. Dallas: Hyatt Press, 1998. Pages 35-54.

     •   Qualben, Lars P. A History of the Christian Church. New York: Thomas Nelson, 1933. P. 99.

❑   LECTURE OUTLINE:

I.   OVERVIEW

    A.   The Shift from Spirit-life and Biblical
        Equality to Institutionalism and Patriarchy
        Increased in the Latter Second Century.

    B.   Montanism, the Church's First Revival, Was
        the Turning Point Downward for Women
        and for the Church.

    C.   As Outward Form, Ritual, and Political
        Control Displaced the Holy Spirit, Christian
        Women Were Increasingly Oppressed and
        Subjugated to Men.

II.   THE RISE OF INSTITUTIONALISM—BAD
       NEWS FOR WOMEN

Principle: In the early Church, institutionalism
crept in at the expense of Spirit-life, and to the
extent that the leadership of the Holy Spirit is lost,
women are marginalized.

pp. 39-42

    A.   What Is Institutionalism?

        1.   Definition: Institutionalism is an
            emphasis on organization at the
            expense of other factors, and in the
            case of the Church, it means that
            human control displaces the
            leadership of the Holy Spirit.

        2.   One symptom of institutionalism is
            hierarchical (chain-of-command)
            rule, or the domination of some over
            others.

            a.   It may take the form of
                patriarchy, the domination of
                men over women.

            b.   It may take the form of
                matriarchy, the domination of
                women over men.

3.   Another symptom of institutionalism is the division of Christians into two classes: a ruling class called "clergy" (<u>kleros</u>) and a subservient class called "laity" (<u>laos</u>).   pp. 39-40

    a.   This is a misuse of these two NT terms since both are consistently used to refer to all the people of God with all believers being called both <u>kleros</u> (1 Pet. 5:4) and "the people of God" (<u>laos</u>).

    b.   The institutional trend prevailed and the term <u>clergy</u> (<u>kleros</u>) was the term used for those who ruled over the <u>laity</u> (<u>laos</u>).

B.   Advance of Institutionalism in the Early Church   p. 40

1.   By the fourth century, the political, clerical ruling class had displaced the charismatic leadership of the Spirit.

2.   In the early 300s, the Roman emperor, Constantine, moved Christianity toward becoming the official religion of the state.

    a.   The Church moved toward a highly developed patriarchal system of government, derived not from the teachings of Jesus, but identical in structure to the political empire of Rome.

    b.   The outward forms of office, ritual, and sacraments displaced personal, Spirit-empowered relationship and the ministry of the Spirit as the Self-disclosure of God to and through His people.

      c.   With this shift and quenching of the Spirit came the stifling, subordination, and marginalization of women.

  3.   Ignatius (A.D. 67-c.a. 107) contributed to the trend toward institutionalism.

pp. 40-42

      a.   He pressed for centralized control over the numerous house churches of a city or region, and to do so he designed a church structure like the civil government.

See chart on following page.

      b.   In this structure, he claimed new authority for the bishop, seeing that person in the sense of the <u>civitas</u> or mayor with the sole authority to rule over all the congregations in a locality.

      c.   History demonstrates that the institutional trend advocated by Ignatius prevailed, and in, the idea of <u>bishop</u> became an office with regal status.

      d.   For those who embraced this emphasis on organizational structure, spiritual authority was no longer seen as residing in the person with the spiritual gift, but in the one occupying the ecclesiastical office.

C.   Summary

Historians agree that the institutionalization of the early Church was accompanied by the demise of the charismatic gifts. This loss of spiritual power was accompanied by the marginalization and subjugation of women.

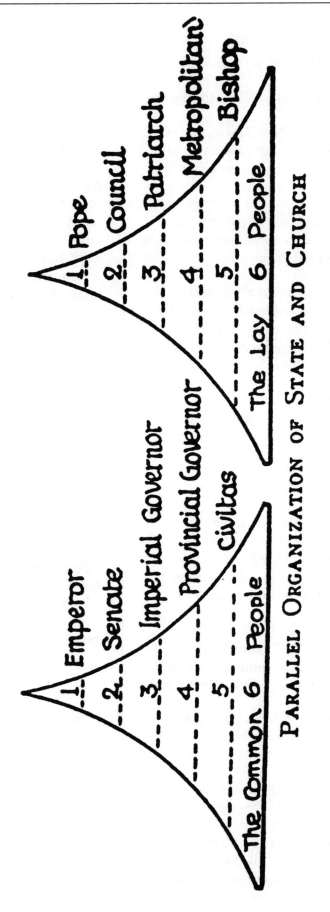

PARALLEL ORGANIZATION OF STATE AND CHURCH

This diagram is taken from Lars P. Qualben, A History of the Christian Church (New York: Thomas Nelson and Sons, 1933), 99.

III.   MONTANISM: THE FIRST REVIVAL
        AND ITS SIGNIFICANCE FOR WOMEN

    A.   The Church's First Revival Was <u>Montanism</u>.

        1.   This revival of New Testament
              Christianity was both a reaction to
              institutionalism as well as a response
              to the Holy Spirit.

        2.   This move of God began through
              Montanus and two women named
              Maxmilla and Prisca.

        3.   It originated in Phrygia in Asia
              Minor but spread quickly especially
              to North Africa where Tertullian
              (A.D. 160-240), joined the movement
              around A.D. 200.

        4.   The Montanists believed ministry
              arose from the possession of spiritual
              gifts, not ecclesiastical appointment.

            a.   This released into ministry
                  both men and women.

            b.   This also challenged the
                  authority claimed by the
                  Church hierarchs who said
                  the right to minister came
                  from the institution.

        5.   The renewal so threatened the
              hierarchs of the Church that the
              Council of Constantinople (A.D. 381)
              denounced these believers as pagans.

    B.   Montanism Was Good News for Women.

        1.   Women were elevated because the
              criterion for service was the
              empowering of the Spirit, the
              anointing and <u>charismata</u>.

        2.   Both women and men were
              encouraged to be filled with the Holy
              Spirit and to spread the Good News.

---

pp. 42-43

Beginning with Augustus
Neander in the 19th
century, modern scholars
have often attempted to
identify Montanism with
the mystery religious
cults of Asia Minor. This
view, however, is by no
means universally
accepted even among
non-Pentecostal scholars.

The earliest critics of
Montanism did not
condemn them on the
basis of doctrine, but
rather on the basis of the
ecstatic manner in which
they delivered their
prophecies. Eddie L.
Hyatt explores this in his
paper entitled
<u>Montanism: Pagan
Frenzy or Pentecostal
Fervor</u>? He provides
solid evidence that the
Montanists were, in fact,
Spirit-filled, revival
people.

p. 43

p. 43-44

3.   Tertullian, who, in his early writings spoke vehemently against women, joined the Montanists and modified his views, speaking respectfully of Prisca, Maxmilla, and a "gifted sister" in his congregation.   p. 44

C.   Montanist Women Were Detested by the Institutional Church.   p. 44-46

    1.   Montanist opponents railed against the Montanist women, especially against Maxmilla and Prisca.

        a.   They accused them of being filled with a "sham spirit" and of chattering "crazily and wildly."

        b.   They also falsely accused them of leaving their husbands and of prophesying for financial gain.

    2.   Evidence indicates that these railings were untrue.

IV.   STRATEGIC RESULTS

A.   The Church's rejection of revival through Montanism accelerated its own progress toward institutionalism.   p. 46

    1.   Class distinction between clergy and laity in the Church's governing structure increased.

    2.   As organizational structure and ritual displaced the Spirit, women were pushed down.

    3.   The developing clerical class was clearly for men only.

B.   The rejection of the Montanists brought a corresponding suppression of women.   p. 46

C.   These developments would necessitate the   p. 47
        formulation of theologies to justify both the
        absence of Spiritual power in the Church
        and the secondary status of women.

D.   Throughout the centuries, the Holy Spirit   p. 47
        has continued to renew true believers, and
        with these renewals have come efforts by
        the Spirit to democratize the Church and to
        reinstate the egalitarian status of women.

E.   The Church has never fully recovered from   p. 47
        the rejection of the Spirit and women in the
        Montanist Revival.

APPLICATION AND ENRICHMENT PROJECTS

1.   In Charismatic groups today, can you identify the governing structure similar to that of Rome? If so, which groups follow this pattern? When did it happen?

2.   What can you discover about why these groups adopted hierarchical forms of government?

3.   In these institutions, what is the status of women in the home and in the Church? Is it the same or different? What is the basis on which they determine the status of women in the home and in the Church?

4.   Are these institutions patriarchal or matriarchal or simply hierarchical without concern for gender in leadership? If these hierarchical groups, who occupies the highest office? Why?

5.   Think about what ministry is according to Jesus and the New Testament writings after the Day of Pentecost. How does it differ from the idea of ministry in the Old Testament? Why is it different? Begin to formulate your own understanding of ministry and be willing to commit to it based on knowledge.

6.   Continue to be alert for reference helps regarding this lesson. Add these titles to your bibliography, books to your library, and articles to your files.

7.   Review the lesson and do the Study and Review section on the next page.

8.   Write a one-page (250-word) essay on the material in this lesson, placing emphasis on the part(s) that were most interesting or useful to you. Your paper should be double-spaced and should be typed in 12-point, Times Roman font. This will constitute page 3 of a paper that may be considered part of a final grade in this course.

FOR STUDY AND REVIEW

PART I

Based on the teaching in this lesson, indicate if the following statements are true or false by inserting a T or an F in the space provided.

1.   ___ Throughout the centuries, the Holy Spirit has continued to renew true believers, and with these renewals have come efforts by the Spirit to democratize the Church and to reinstate the egalitarian status of women.

2.   ___ To the extent that institutionalism replaced the leadership of the Holy Spirit, women were elevated to equality with men.

3.   ___ In the New Testament, all believers are called both "clergy" (kleros) and "laity" (laos).

4.   ___ The Church's rejection of revival through Montanism resulted in a corresponding elevation of women.

5.   ___ The shift from Spirit-life and Biblical equality to institutionalism increased in the latter second century.

PART II

Complete the sentences by selecting the best answers from the following list:

** Maxmilla ** institutionalism ** Montanism ** Roman Empire **
** Montanists ** human control ** Tertullian ** Prisca **

1.   _____ was the Church's first revival.

2.   In the early Church, _____ crept in at the expense of Spirit-life.

3.   The Church moved toward a patriarchal system of government derived, not from the teachings of Jesus, but identical in structure to the _____ _____.

4.   Institutionalism is an emphasis on organization in which _____ _____ displaces the leadership of the Holy Spirit.

5.   _____, who, in his early writings spoke vehemently against women, joined the _____ and modified his views, speaking respectfully of _____, _____, and a "gifted sister" in his congregation.

LESSON 4

What Did the Church Say about Women?

LESSON 4
What Did the Church Say about Women?

❑ THEME: The egalitarian message of Jesus about women was "written out" of traditional theology when the institutionalized Church adopted the ideas of Church fathers who were heavily influenced by misogynous and patriarchal, pagan presuppositions.

❑ PURPOSE: To discover, by a brief overview of relevant Church history, the source and development of the Church's traditional teaching about women.

❑ OBJECTIVES:

1. To reveal the pagan presuppositions influencing the Church fathers as they laid the foundations of the Church's traditional theology of womanhood.

2. To point out the misogyny of the medieval church.

3. To cite the patriarchal attitudes of the Reformers.

4. To show the effect of the misogyny and hierarchy of the English Reformation on biblical interpretation regarding womanhood.

❑ TEXTBOOK READING: Chapter 5-8, pp. 49-80

❑ SUGGESTED READING AND TEACHING RESOURCES:

- Bristow, John Temple. What Paul Really Said About Women. New York: Harper and Row, 1988. Pp. 3-5.

- Donaldson, James and Alexander Roberts, Ed. Ante-Nicene Fathers. 10 Vols. 1885 Reprint. Peabody, MA: Hendrickson, 1995. See textbook for specific references.

- Mickelsen, Alvera and Berkeley. "Does Male Dominance Tarnish Our Translations?" Christianity Today. Oct. 5, 1979: 23-27.

- Schmidt, Alvin John. Veiled and Silenced: How Culture Shaped Sexist Theology Macon: Mercer University Press, 1989. Pp. 163.

- Storkey, Elaine. "Nuns, Witches and Patriarchy." Contributions to Christian Feminism. London: Christian Impact, 1995.

- Tucker, Ruth A. and Walter Liefeld. Daughters of the Church. Grand Rapids: Zondervan, 1987.

❑ LESSON OUTLINE:

I.   THE FOUNDATIONS AND DEVELOPMENT OF
      THE TRADITIONAL THEOLOGY OF
      WOMANHOOD

      A.   Principles

            1.   The attitudes of the church fathers,
                  molded by pagan ideas about
                  women, influenced how they
                  interpreted Scriptures about women
                  and about male/female relationships.
                  Their theological formulations
                  emerged as the traditional or
                  orthodox theology—or acceptable
                  way of thinking about things—and
                  generally disregarded Jesus' teaching
                  about women.

            2.   It is possible to find a few scattered
                  positive remarks about individual
                  women in the writings of the Church
                  fathers, but their attitude and remarks
                  are overwhelmingly negative, and
                  these prevail in their doctrinal
                  formulations about womanhood.

      B.   Influential Elements

            1.   Pagan presuppositions declared
                  womanhood to be evil, inferior,
                  unequal, and unclean,
                  presuppositions totally foreign to
                  Jesus' message about women.

Schmidt's Veiled and
Silenced provides an
excellent study of this.

            2.   Two Greek philosophers, Socrates
                  (ca. 470-399 B.C.) and Aristotle
                  (384-322 B.C.), influenced the
                  development of thought among early
                  Church leaders.

Bristow's What Paul
Really Said about
Women explains this.

See p. 50 of textbook.

            3.   Theological formulation lacked Holy
                  Spirit influence.

            4.   Human traditions prevailed over
                  biblical principles.

5.   Political and personal agendas of Church leaders denied women equality with men.

II.   PERCEPTIONS OF WOMANHOOD AMONG THE CHURCH FATHERS

A.   Clement of Alexandria (*ca.* A.D. 150-220)   p. 51

B.   Tertullian (A.D. 160-240)   pp. 51-52

C.   Origen (A.D. 185-254)   p. 52

D.   Ambrose of Milan (A.D. 340-397)   pp. 52-53

E.   Augustine (A.D. 354-430)   p. 53

F.   Cyril of Alexandria (d. 444)   p. 54

G.   Chrysostom (A.D. 347-407)   p. 54-55

H.   Jerome (A.D. 340 - 420)   pp. 55-56

I.   Summary Statement   p. 56.

III.   WOMANHOOD IN THE MEDIEVAL CHURCH   p. 57

Life was especially difficult for women in the Middle Ages. They were valued only as "wombs," "workers," and objects of male gratification in a highly patriarchal society. The attitude of the institutional Church contributed to this hardship. As the institution exercised increasing authority, it imposed celibacy on its clergy and their wives were suddenly cast out and demonized. The witchcraft craze led to innocent old peasant women and midwives being burned at the stake for alleged witchcraft.

A.   The Beguines Were Bold Women of Spirit.

1.   Beguines were Christian women in a movement that originated in the Netherlands in the twelfth century.

Broader discussions of the various opportunities for women in the Church of this era should be read. Suggestions include: 1) Tucker and Liefeld's "Medieval Catholicism: Nuns, 'Heretics,' and Mystics," in their Daughters of the Church (pp. 129-169); and 2) McLaughlin's "Women, Power and the Pursuit of Holiness in Medieval Christianity" in Women of Spirit (pp. 99-130).

2.   Because they were not sanctioned by the papacy, the Church condemned them and burned them at the stake.

B.   Thomas Aquinas'(d. 1247) Horrific Influence on Womanhood.   pp. 58-59

    1.   Aquinas' influence reaches far because he was the authoritative teacher of Roman theology who systematized Christian beliefs.

    2.   Aquinas' influential teachings were highly misogynous.

        a.   He drew from Augustine and Aristotle, and so "the Greek deprecation of women became solidly infused within Christian theology."

        b   He believed that women are "defective and misbegotten," as well as totally inferior.

    3.   Aquinas prompted the Inquisition and the burning of women as witches.

C.   Other Leaders Held Misogynous Attitudes.

    1.   Odo of Cluny, in the twelfth century, wrote, "To embrace a woman is to embrace a sack of manure."   p. 59

    2.   Bonaventura conceded that woman is "man's equal in nature, grace, and glory," but was more in agreement with Aristotle than with the Bible.   p. 59

D.   The Medieval Church Sanctioned Wife-Beating.   pp. 59-60

    1.   The Church taught that wife-beating was "chastisement" for disobedience and exhorted men to beat their wives and wives to kiss the rod that beat them.

2.   It was justified by the "headship"
        supposedly espoused by 1 Cor. 11:3.

5.   Friar Cherubino's 15th century <u>Rule</u>   Read the Rule of
        <u>of Marriage</u> encouraged wife-abuse.   Marriage on p. 60.

E.   The Church Moved from Misogyny and
        Fear to Rejection of Women to Burning over
        a Million Women at the Stake as Witches.

        1.   A series of papal reforms intensified   p. 60
                the persecution of women.

        2.   Papal couriers traveled from town to   p. 61
                town proclaiming the evils of female
                sexuality.

        3.   <u>The Witches' Hammer</u> (1486), a   p. 61
                book by two German theologians, is
                a landmark document about witches,
                womanhood, and their torture.

        4.   The Church is responsible for over a
                million women being tried for the
                heresy of witchcraft and burned at
                the stake.

F.   The Question for the Pentecostal and   pp. 62-63
        Charismatic Believer Is: Were These
        Women Witches or Spirit-filled Christians?

        1.   In the <u>Roman Ritual</u> (A.D. 1000), the
                Roman Church had designated
                speaking in tongues as the chief
                evidence of demonic possession
                among the common folk.

        2.   Any supernatural phenomena among
                the common people was looked upon
                as sorcery and witchcraft.

        3.   Some "witches" were Spirit-filled
                believers who refused to submit to
                the Church's concerted effort to
                control the people.

        4.   Some of these women were innocent,
                elderly women.

5.   Some were punished because they   p. 63
        knew more than the men about
        gynecology, and this threatened the
        authority of the Church leaders.

G.   Conclusion

    1.   The thinking of the men who shaped   p. 63-64
            medieval theology and practice was
            hostile toward women and the
            charismata among the masses.

    2.   Their chain-of-being perspective
            purported that men were of higher
            substance, greater value, and more
            noble function than women.

    3.   The Medieval Church's theology of
            womanhood was warped by pagan
            philosophy, misogyny, and
            hierarchical world view. Its theology
            of womanhood was, therefore, highly
            unbiblical, yet much of it still
            provides the context in which we
            interpret biblical womanhood.

IV.   WOMANHOOD IN THE REFORMATION   Ch. 7 begins here.

A.   The Reformation (1517-1648) put the Bible   p. 65
        in the hands of the people, but it did little to
        revive Jesus' message about womanhood.

    1.   The chain-of-being perception,   See John Knox quote on
            which attributed superiority to man   p. 65.
            and inferiority to women, prevailed,
            and since the issue of authority was
            the chief concern of the Reformers,
            women remained secondary,
            subordinate, and subject to men.

    2.   The conviction that only the male
            can represent Jesus in institutional
            church offices remained firmly
            intact.

B.   Martin Luther's (1483-1546) Three Biblical Principles Had Implications for the Theology of Womanhood.   p. 65

1.   The Priesthood of All Believers. Did "all believers," in fact, include women—or just men?   pp. 65-66

a.   Luther had been an Augustinian monk, and would have been in taught the notion of woman's inferior and evil nature.

b.   He believed that "woman was much more liable to superstition and occultism."

c.   He appealed to the alleged rule of female silence (1 Cor. 14:34; 1 Tim. 2:11).

d.   He held women responsible for the Fall, and therefore retained the concept of female subjugation.

e.   After several years, he decided, "If it happens that no man is present a woman can take charge and preach before others as far as she is able."

2.   Sola fide. This declared that salvation is by grace through faith.   p. 66

This doctrine relieved men of the vain burden of salvation by works, but did it include women? Was there equal redemption available for all? Were women wholly human and could they be wholly saved?

3.   Sola scriptura. This makes the Bible, rather than tradition or the rulings of the institutional Church, authoritative for faith and practice, but authority was really not derived from Scripture itself, but from a person's   p. 66

interpretation of Scripture. (And it must be noted that interpretation continued to be skewed by misogyny, hierarchical worldview, and the perennial influence of Greek philosophy. In other words, the starting point for interpreting the Bible continued to be biased against women.)

C.   John Calvin (1509-1564) Stressed the Idea of Institutions with Authority Delegated in Patriarchal Fashion.

Read Calvin's quote on pp. 67-68.

1.   It is said that he did not derive his system of theology from Augustine, but from the Bible; nevertheless, it is a fact that he allowed the writings of Augustine to confirm his theology.

2.   His teaching on sovereignty, predestination, and government reinforces authoritative male headship/female subjugation, predetermined roles based on gender, and institutionalism with its hierarchical/patriarchal model.

3.   He retained the prevailing, negative theology of womanhood derived from the church fathers and common in the medieval church.

4.   According to Calvin, God governs by delegated authority, which, some say, is observable in the Godhead.

p. 68

   a.   Added to this is the idea that God is male and the metaphor of God as "Father," and this means that a man, who is a father, represents God and therefore has authority of the highest order.

Read the quotation by John Yoder on p. 69.

What is a "metaphor"?

   b.   This also implies that a woman can never ascend to this kind of authority since

We must be careful not to make God in our image!

she can never be "father" and
so, represent Father God.

  c. This thinking falls short of
    what the Bible teaches
    because God is a Spirit and
    transcends gender.

D. Protestantism's General Rejection of the   pp. 69-71
   Charismatic Activity of the Spirit Denied the
   Elevating, Equalizing Effect of the Spirit.

  1. Although Luther made some room p. 69
    for miracles and the charismata in his
    personal life, he denounced
    charismatic manifestations,
    especially those among the
    Anabaptists and Roman Catholics.

  2. Although Calvin has been called the p. 69
    "Theologian of the Spirit," his anti-
    charismatic stance was fed by
    Aristotle and Aquinas whose
    influence "left no room for the direct
    spiritual experience with the Spirit."

  3. The rejection of the charismata— This is a very significant
    which could be defined as a   principle.
    restriction on the Holy Spirit—
    appears to coincide with a restriction
    on women. Where the Holy Spirit is
    silenced, it appears that women also
    tend to be silenced.

  4. Evangelicals and other Reformed
    Groups who hold to Luther and
    Calvin tend to promote a theology of
    gender inequality.

E. Anabaptist Women Received Mixed   pp. 72-74
   Messages.

  1. Pentecostalism "is in our century the p. 72
    closest parallel to what Anabaptism
    was in the sixteenth century."

    a. They believed in the active
      presence of the Holy Spirit

               including divine revelation and illumination of Scripture.

       b.   They also believed in both the priesthood and prophethood of all believers.

   2.   Recognition of the anointing of the Spirit on Anabaptist women resulted in many Anabaptist women preachers.   p. 73

   3.   Women were, however, highly restricted, domestically.   Read examples in the textbook on pp. 73-74.

F.   Conclusion   p. 74

   1.   For women, the period of Reformation continued to be a time of great oppression.

   2.   They remained at the bottom in the hierarchical mindset of the Church.

   3.   Domestically, women continued to be secondary and subordinate.

   4.   Theologically, hope flickered with the formulation of the doctrines of the priesthood and prophethood of all believers, but these doctrines served primarily the purposes of a patriarchal culture.

V.   WOMANHOOD IN THE ENGLISH REFORMATION   Chapter 8 begins here. Pp. 75-80

A.   Events in England in the 1600s Helped Establish Popular Notions about "Church," and about Man as "High Priest" and "Head" of the Home.

   1.   Two basic questions alert us to a problem in this formulation.

       a.   <u>Is the home the basic unit of the Church</u>? Where did Jesus say that the home is the   p. 75

unit of the Church? Where did you learn this? Why?

b. <u>Is a married man the "high priest" and ruler of the home</u>? Where did Jesus (or the New Testament) say that this? Where did you learn this? Why?

pp. 75-76

2. How did Jesus define "church"?

p. 75

a. What did Jesus say? "Where two or three have come together in my Name, there I am in the midst of them (Mt. 18:20, Author's translation).

b. Irenaus affirmed Jesus' teaching about what constitutes the Church of which Jesus spoke when he said, "Where the [true] church is, there is the Spirit; and where the Spirit of God is, there is the church."

p. 75

3. How Did the English Church Progress Toward These Beliefs?

p. 76

a. The Thirty Years' War (1618-1648) inflamed the European continent and spread to England where the state Church of England swayed between Roman Catholicism and Protestantism.

b. Henry VIII (1509-47) severed the English church from Rome (1534) and declared the king to be "the supreme head of the church of England."

c. This reflected an austere, hierarchical world view, and it reinforced in the English-speaking world, a form of church government patterned after state government.

  d. In addition, the English kings held to the "divine right of kings," that is, the God-ordained right of the monarch to ultimate authority.

                  Be sure to research this idea of the "divine right" of kings in an encyclopedia.

  e. It is interesting to note that it was in such a climate of struggle of power and control that the Authorized King James Version of the Bible (1611) was translated.

                  pp. 76-77

B. Significant Factors Surround the Highly Influential King James Version of the Bible.

  1. King James I (b. 1566, ruled 1603-25) commissioned the 1611 Authorized Version of the Bible to pacify the Puritans, rally political support, and consolidate his power base.

  2. He apparently hated women and vowed to suppress them.

  3. Is it possible that the King James Version (KJV) could have been influenced by misogynous sentiments? A couple of examples clearly illustrate that such tampering did, in fact, occur.

    a. In Acts 18:26, the KJV translators reverse the order of Priscilla and Aquila. In the Greek text, Priscilla comes first. In the KJV, however, Aquila comes first, a reversal that shows deference to the husband.

                  p. 77

    b. The KJV translation of the Greek word hesychia also

                  p. 78

reveals evidence of anti-woman sentiments. 1 Tim. 2:11 reads, "Let the women learn in silence." 2 Thes. 3:12 reads, "with quietness they work and eat." The phrases "in silence" and "with quietness" are translations of the same Greek word <u>hesychia</u>. In a context referring to women, the KJV translators used "in silence," but in a context referring to men, they used "in quietness."

    c.   Phoebe (Rom. 16:1), Paul (1 Cor. 3:5), Timothy (1 Tim. 4:6), Epaphras (Col. 1:7), Tychicus (Col. 4:7; Eph. 6:21), and Apollos (1 Cor. 3:5) are all referred to as <u>diakonos</u> in the Greek text. The KJV translates <u>diakonos</u> as "deacon" and "minister"— except on one occasion! In the case of Phoebe, <u>diakonos</u> becomes "a servant" instead of a "deacon" or "minister."   p. 78

C.   Home: "Little Kingdom" and "Little Church" with the Man as Ruler of Both.

    1.   The issue at stake was control over the masses and women preachers.   pp. 78-79

    2.   To establish this control, the religious hierarchy asserted with great intensity the idea of authoritative male headship in the home.

        a.   The man was required by Church and State to manage his wife, children, and workers.

        b.   Puritans described family as a little church and a little   p. 79

commonwealth, a place to train servants and women in subjugation.

3.	The Puritans, following Calvin, established human government on the basis of what they believed were three divinely ordained institutions: the state, the church, and the home, which were divinely ruled by means of delegated authority:	p. 79

	a.	In the same way that the head-of-the-state supposedly derived authority from God, the head-of-the-church supposedly derived authority from God, and the head-of-the-home supposedly derived authority from God.

	b.	The head (incorrectly defined as "ruler") of each of these had to be a man because, according to their theology, God had, according to their beliefs, predestined man to rule and woman to serve.

4.	When the monarchy was reinstated in 1660, the idea of "the divine right of kings" remained in tact.	pp. 79-80

	a.	The English king was now authoritative in the state as God's designated ruler of the earthly kingdom, and as high priest, that is as God's representative earthly ruler of the Church. (No where in Scripture is this taught.)

	b.	This notion of "divine order" continued to be extended to the home which was already "a little church and a little common-wealth," but now it became "a little church" and "a little kingdom."

  c. The home was to be seen as a little kingdom where the man was to rule as king of "his castle" in the same way as the King of England was to rule the state.

  d. Furthermore, the home was also to be seen as a little church where the man was to rule as high priest in the same way that the King was to rule the Church of England.

  e. So the man was now king and priest of the home with woman as subject both politically and religiously.

D. Conclusion   p. 80

This is probably the first time that the link was made between the two separate "roles" of <u>head-of-home</u> and <u>priest-of-the-home</u> so commonly taught among Pentecostal/Charismatics today. Yet nowhere in the NT are these roles taught; nowhere in the NT are they linked; and nowhere in the NT is the male given responsibility to dominate the female.

VI. SUMMARY

A. The Church fathers laid a faulty foundation for a theology of biblical womanhood because the primary influences on their thinking were the pagan presuppositions that women are evil, inferior, unequal, and unclean, and by the perspectives of Platonic and Aristotelian philosophy,

B. The Medieval period brought increased oppression, abuse, persecution, and execution for women, especially through the papacy and Aquinas (1125-1274) who systematized Roman theology using Aristotelian philosophy, thus reinforcing the idea of male primacy in the root system of traditional, orthodox theology.

C.   During the Reformation, women continued to be oppressed with only a faint hope coming through the priesthood and prophethood of all believers, since these primarily served the purposes of a patriarchal Church.

D.   During the English Reformation, the formidable link was made between the two separate Calvinistic-Augustinian "roles" of head-of-home and priest-of-the-home so commonly taught among Pentecostal/Charismatics today.

E.   Even today among Spirit-oriented believers, sexist theology, rooted so much in pagan presuppositions of womanhood, continues to provide a misogynous starting point for biblical interpretation regarding women.

APPLICATION AND ENRICHMENT PROJECTS

1. Using a concordance or other Bible study aids, find passages that indicate that God is Spirit. Think about this until you are persuaded that it is important not to make God in our image with the idea of gender.

2. Read Alvera and Berkeley Mickelsen's article, "Does Male Dominance Tarnish Our Translations?" Christianity Today. Oct. 5, 1979: 23-27.

3. Read and respond briefly to the following passage by Susan C. Hyatt on the "Blame, Shame, and Tame" theology of womanhood.

    Throughout the centuries, the Church's theology of womanhood has been characterized by blame, a trait that has made it easy to shame and tame women. This theology of "blame" says that women are responsible for the fall of man and are, therefore, evil, inferior, unequal, and unclean. This unbiblical thinking must be rooted out, not merely covered over by convenient modifications.

    The tactic of shame is often the first line of aggression used against a woman who might be forgetting her "proper place." Shaming occurs in many different ways, but one common approach is defamation through labeling. For example, such a woman would immediately be termed a feminist with a full spectrum of negative undertones intended. Another is the designation Jezebel. This slur is currently popular among some revival people who are quick to protect traditionally male turf from gifted women leaders. The patriarchs applaud submissive women who teach male authoritative headship and female subordination and who denounce their egalitarian sisters as "Jezebels." Many believing women, unsure of themselves and ignorant of their theological rights, shy away from behavior that would prompt such defamation.

    The theology of blame has also made it relatively easy to tame highly motivated women of God. Patriarchs accomplish this through doctoral corollaries. For example, based on the faulty premise that women alone were responsible for the fall, doctrines of unilateral female submission and female subjugation in all venues of life have been firmly established as norms. To break these norms is to invite the sordid reputation of being rebellious with the quick reminder that rebellion is as the sin of witchcraft. Indeed, these doctrines serve to tame women and are do not reflect the teaching of Jesus. This orthodox theological context of "blame, shame, and tame" is not biblical, logical, or acceptable.

4. Has the information in this lesson influenced your thinking. If so, how?

5. Seek out an avowed feminist, particularly one who is well-educated, and ask her how she feels about the church and why. Do not try to convert her at this point. Simply listen with an ear to gain knowledge of her perspective.

6. Write a one-page (250-word) essay on the material in this lesson, placing emphasis on the part(s) that were most interesting or useful to you. Your paper should be double-spaced and should be typed in 12-point, Times Roman font. This will constitute page 4 of a paper that may be considered part of a final grade in this course.

FOR STUDY AND REVIEW

PART I

Based on the teaching in this lesson, indicate if the following statements are true or false by inserting a T or an F in the space provided.

1. ___ The prevailing attitude of the Church fathers toward women was heavily influenced by the pagan idea that women are evil, unclean, inferior, and unequal.

2. ___ The Church of the Middle Ages taught that wife-beating was "chastisement" for disobedience and exhorted men to beat their wives and wives to kiss the rod that beat them..

3. ___ None of the women burned at the stake were Spirit-filled Christians.

4. ___ Protestantism's general rejection of the charismatic activity of the Spirit denied the elevating, equalizing effect of the Spirit.

5. ___ The Reformation revived the message of Jesus about womanhood.

6. ___ The Bible teaches that a man is the "high priest" and ruler of the home.

7. ___ Jesus taught that the basic unit of the Church is the home.

8. ___ The idea that the man is the ruler of the home was promoted by King James and the English Reformation as means of controlling society.

9. ___ "Priesthood of all believers" includes women.

10. ___ Political and personal agendas of Church leaders denied women equality.

PART II

Complete the sentences by selecting the best answers from the following list:

** witches ** Socrates * Beguines ** Roman Ritual ** Aristotle ** Aquinas **

1. Two Greek philosophers, _____ and _____, influenced the development of thinking about womanhood among early Church leaders.

2. The _____ were bold women of the Spirit during the Middle Ages.

3. _____, the official theologian of the Roman Catholic Church in the 13th century, believed that women "are defective and misbegotten" and totally inferior.

4. In the _____ _____ (A.D. 1000), the Roman Church designated speaking in tongues as the chief evidence of demonic possession among the common folk.

5. Some _____ were Spirit-filled believers who refused to submit to the Church's effort to control the people.

LESSON 5

What Was the Holy Spirit Saying about Women?

LESSON 5

What Was the Holy Spirit Saying About Women?

❑ THEME: The recognition by the Early Friends (1650-1690) and the Early Methodists (1739-1760) of the Holy Spirit's dwelling equally in and upon both women and men brought about an elevation of womanhood, and in the case of the Friends, an egalitarian life style.

❑ PURPOSE: To provide significant historical evidence that when believers are led by the Spirit, they move toward an egalitarian understanding of Christian lifestyle that breaks with traditional hierarchy and the traditional theology of womanhood.

❑ OBJECTIVES:

1. To become aware of the work of the Spirit on behalf of women among the Early Quaker and Methodist Revivals.

2. To look at important, leading players in each revival.

3. To examine the key theological beliefs that led to equality among the Friends and to inclusivism among the Methodists.

4. To confront the cost of standing for biblical truth in religious culture.

5. To consider strategic long-term effects for women.

❑ TEXTBOOK READING: Chapter 9 and 10, pp. 83-144.

❑ SUGGESTED READING AND TEACHER RESOURCES:

• Hyatt, Susan. "The Good Fruit Remains: The Friends and Their Profound Impact." The Hyatt Quarterly. Summer 1997: 5, 8-9. This is included with this lesson.

• Hyatt, Susan. Where Are My Susannas? Dallas: Hyatt Press, 1997.

• Chilcote, John Wesley. John Wesley and the Women Preachers of Early Methodism. Metuchen: Scarecrow, 1991.

• Fell, Margaret. Womens Speaking Justified. 1979 Reprint by the Augustan Reprint Society; London, 1667. Available in the Huntingdon Library (Shelf Mark: 94232; Wing F-643) and in the Special Collections Room at Gordon Conwell Library.

• Penn, William. "The Preface. " Vol. 1. The Works of George Fox. 8 Vols. 1706 Reprint. New York: AMS Press, 1975. This is well worth the effort of locating and reading.

❏ LECTURE OUTLINE:	QUESTIONS, NOTES, AND TEXTBOOK REFERENCES

I.   OVERVIEW   p. 83

   A.   By the mid-1600s in England, with the Bible now in the hands of the people and the yoke of Rome broken, the long road of liberation and elevation of women began in earnest.

   B.   In this work of the Spirit, oppression and control of one person over another would be discarded in varying degrees, and patterns of equality, respect, and mutuality would be modeled.

   C.   This plan is obvious in a remarkable way among the Early Friends (1650-90), and to a lesser extent among the Early Methodists (1739-60), and in varying degrees in the revival movements of the 19th Century.

   D.   This egalitarianism merged briefly in Early Pentecostalism (1901-05).

This date could be extended to 1907 or 1909 in order to point to the egalitarianism at Azusa Street. Parham's influence is arguably the primary cause of the egalitarianism there.

   E.   Three main features mark each of these movements:

      1.   They were grounded in Scripture.

      2.   They were orchestrated and empowered by the Holy Spirit.

      3.   They were facilitated by courageous men and women of faith.

II.   BIBLICAL WOMANHOOD AND THE EARLY FRIENDS (1650-1690)

Chapter 9 begins here. pp. 83-130

   A.   In England, in about 1650, a group known as the Religious Society of Friends or Quakers arose and began promoting biblical equality.

p. 83; pp. 93-97

      1.   "Quakerism was fundamentally a way of life, not a system of thought or doctrine."

2.   They were missions-minded and spread the Gospel far and wide.   pp. 83-84

3.   They were the fastest growing movement in the western world.

4.   These Spirit-oriented, Bible-believing, revival people were the first major, influential advocates of biblical equality since New Testament days or perhaps since the days of the Montanist revival.

B.   George Fox (1624-1691) was the itinerant preacher regarded as its founder.   pp. 85-90

He was also a man of considerable influence. In fact, Penn notes, "Some erroneously accused him of seeking dominion over people's consciences . . . because he was held in high esteem by many." But, says Penn, "He exercised no authority but over evil."   p. 89

C.   Quakers was severely persecuted by the Anglicans and Puritans.   p. 88

1.   They were imprisoned for:

a.   Refusing to pays tithes to support local priests.

b.   Refusing to doff their hats for social superiors.

c.   Refusing to be married by the priests.

d.   Interrupting church services.

e.   Refusing to serve in the army.

D.   A number of experiences influenced Fox to work toward equality, not only generally in society, but also on behalf of women.

1.   When he encountered men who believed that women had no souls, "no more than a goose," he reminded them of Mary's words: "My soul doth magnify the Lord" (Lk. 1:46).

p. 89

2.   In 1648, in a meeting in a "steeplehouse," he was angered when he observed a woman ask a question only to be told by the priest that he did not permit women to speak in church.

3.   He recognized and respected the anointing on women of faith.

E.   Margaret Fell was a major player who helped assure stability in the Society.

pp. 90-93, p. 87

1.   A former Anglican gentry, Margaret Askew Fell, joined the company of Friends in 1652 and became a formative influence.

2.   Fell's major contribution to the movement may have been the stabilizing of the Women's Meetings.

a.   The separate meetings were necessary when women began to exercise their new-found equality in the Society, and it quickly became apparent that they had neither the education nor the experience to exercise that equality.

p. 92

b.   The Women's Meetings served as a forum for the development of their abilities and the skills vital to leadership.

c.   In these gatherings, the women functioned with the knowledge of their equality, and took responsibility for overseeing marriages, regulating the conduct of their members, relieving the needs of the poor, and keeping good accounts and records.

3.   Fell wrote voluminously.   p. 93

    a.   In 1666, she wrote <u>Women Speaking Justified</u>, the first major book written in favor of a female public ministry.   pp. 113-117

    b.   Fell's tracts were translated into Latin, Dutch, and Hebrew and were carried to the Netherlands by Quaker missionaries.

F.   Relevant Aspects of the Fox' Belief System

1.   Fox believed that Jesus Christ was the only legitimate Mediator (1 Tim. 2:5; Heb. 8:6; 9:15; 12:24).   p. 93, 112; 117-119

    a.   Fox denounced outward mediatory elements such as the priesthood, church buildings, sacraments, and regalia, through which, he asserted, the Church controlled its members.   p. 93-94

    b.   He upheld personal, individual responsibility for a direct and intimate relationship with God.

    c.   This threatened the rigid hierarchical social pattern promoted by the state church and Puritans.

2.   Fox believed in gender equality.

3.   The Inner Light was the definitive theological principle (Jn. 1:1-14).   pp. 97-99

4. Those who gave heed to the Inner Light became new creatures in Christ, and received the "Seed of Promise," the Lord Jesus, and were part of the converted community.

p. 97

5. On the basis of Jn. 1:9, in particular, Fox believed that "'there was that of God,' . . . in all men and women everywhere," and this has serious implications.

p. 100

a. The Inner Light gave confidence in evangelism, for it meant that the potential to respond to the Gospel was inherent in every person.

p. 99

b. The Inner Light is what prompted an egalitarian world view for it meant that men and women were indwelt by this same potential from God.

p. 98-99

c. It was the basis of a Christian community in which no one was to dominate another.

d. The Inner Light had a democratizing social effect for it indicated that God was no respecter of persons.

p. 99

6. Penn said the goal of the Inner Light is "to bring things back into their primitive and right order again," and one of these was "to make marriage coincide with the biblical mandate of equal meet-helps."

H. Fox Considered Christ the Only "Head."

pp. 103-104 and pp. 108-113

1. Fox understood that if "headship" involved hierarchy, it was only Christ who could stand above, with all people under only Him, standing on a level field.

2.   He justified this egalitarian principle,   p. 104
        which he believed was demonstrated
        by the Spirit, with biblical evidence
        drawn from Genesis to Revelation.

3.   Fox believed that the indwelling
        Christ is the Husband figure in all
        believers, male and the female
        without distinction, and this liberates
        believers from restrictions previously
        imposed on the basis of gender.

4.   All believers, male and female,
        symbolically become the Wife or
        Bride of Christ.

5.   Fox considers Eph. 5:23-32 the   pp. 105-106
        pivotal paragraph.

        a.   He says that Paul's purpose is
                not to compare the patriarchal
                marriage relationship with
                the relationship of Christ and
                the Church; but rather, his
                purpose is to illustrate the
                mystery of Christ's
                relationship with the Church.

        b.   He contends that Paul
                explains this great mystery by
                means of the metaphor of
                Christ as the male and the
                Church as the female, and all
                members of the true Church
                enjoy this symbolic spiritual
                marriage relationship with
                Christ as the female (Bride)
                with the male
                (Bridegroom/Christ).

        c.   He explains that the pouring   pp. 106-107
                out of the Spirit on all flesh is
                the end-time key event that
                unlocks the great mystery of
                Eph. 5.

6.   Fox argues for the Headship of
Christ and the equality of men and
women, pointing to following: pp. 103-117

   a.   The outpouring of the Spirit
on male and female without
distinction.

   b.   The same indwelling Holy
Spirit equally abiding in both.

   c.   The authority of the Spirit
abiding in both.

   d.   The Spirit as Christ within:
"Christ in you, the hope of
glory" (Col. 1:27).

   e.   The consistent pattern he
describes in Scripture.

   f.   The egalitarian attitudes and
actions of Jesus toward
women.

   g.   The precedent of equality set
by Paul, accurately
understood.

J.   The First Book on Equality for Women: pp. 113-117
Women Speaking Justified (1666).

   1.   Written while Fell served a four-year
stint in prison (1665-8), this book is
a milestone in women's history.

   2.   It was the first apology written by a
Quaker woman defending the right
of women to speak publicly,
prophesy, teach, or preach.

   3.   She asserts that the authority of both
the Gospel and the indwelling Holy
Spirit overrules any purported OT
gender prohibitions of the law or
alleged NT gender restrictions.

   4.   She points out that in creation, God
made no distinction in the
impartation of His image to male and
female.

5.   Fell declares that opposition to women speaking comes from the spirit of darkness and apostasy that had been prevailing in the church for 1200 years.

K.   That God Would Take up Residence in Each Person Was Significant.   pp. 119-120

1.   It meant that each person could gain a new sense of worth.

2.   It meant that each person was responsible to commune directly with God.

3.   It meant that, since God was no respecter of persons in that He gave each one the same potential to respond to Christ, believers were to treat all human beings with equal dignity and respect.

4.   It meant a high motivation for social action.

5.   It meant a shift in the locus of authority from external religious symbols and offices to direct, internal relationship with God.   p. 120

6.   In New England, Puritan persecution reached savage heights, primarily because of the Quaker threat to Puritan patriarchal structures.   pp. 120-121

        a.   The possibility of women preachers was alarming, and anti-Quaker propaganda in Boston linked Quakerism with witchcraft, the common element being the empowerment of women.

        b.   Quaker women were also hung publicly by Puritans in Boston, convicted of insubordination and possible witchcraft.

          c.   Quaker men and women were subjected to public whippings and unthinkable persecution.

L.   Quakers Flourished in Colonial America and Their Legacy Remains Strong.

    1.   The Abolition Movement.

          a.   Sixty years before the Emancipation Proclamation, there was not one Quaker slave-holder in America.   p. 122

          d.   Quaker women were actively and publicly involved in abolition.

    2.   Prison Reform.   p. 124

          a.   Elizabeth Guerney Fry (1780-1845), an English Quaker preacher, is the founder of prison reform.

          b.   Quakers in America initiated important steps in prison reform.

    3.   Indian Affairs.   p. 125

          a.   In America, Quakers were trusted by the Indians, and often represented their interests in treaties.

          b.   Yearly committees established centers where farming skills were taught to Indians on reservations.

    4.   Government Policy.   p. 125

          a.   William Penn (1644-1718), the most noted of Quaker political reformers, played a key role in American colonization.

b.   In 1682, he and eleven other Quakers bought northern New Jersey, and he received the grant of Pennsylvania from the British Crown.

                                                                      p. 125

5.   Co-education.

                                                                      p. 125

a.   George Fox insisted on equal education for boys and girls.

b.   Quakers pioneered higher educational for women in the fields of education, science, and the professions.

M.   Four Religious Movements Reflect the Egalitarianism of Fox   p. 126

1.   Women's Suffrage Movement.   p. 127

a.   This movement was born in the hearts of Spirit-oriented, Bible-believing women.

b.   Quaker women led the seventy year-long struggle that gave American women the right to vote.

c.   Quaker women formulated the Declaration of Sentiments for the Woman's Rights Convention, Seneca Falls, New York, July 19-20, 1848.   This is available at http://www.luminet.net/~tgort/convent.htm, pp3-7.

2.   Early Pentecostalism (1901-1907).

a.   The outpouring occurred at the 1900 Watchnight Service of Bethel Bible School in Topeka, Kansas, a Bible school operated by Charles Parham, Sarah Thistlethwaite-Parham, and Lillian Thistlethwaite.   p. 127

b.   Bethel is usually considered a Holiness institution, but the Thistlethwaite sisters were Friends, and Parham had modified his Methodist-Holiness theology in dialogue with his wife's Quaker grandfather.

c.   While the Parham-Thistlethwaite leadership prevailed (1900-c.a. 1907), egalitarianism characterized the Revival.

d.   As the revival spread beyond the Parham-Thistlethwaite influence, patriarchalism pushed out egalitarianism.

3.   Conservative Evangelical Biblical Equality Movement.   p. 128

a.   A third movement with a Quaker connection is the Evangelical Biblical Equality Movement. Perhaps the most effective group is Christians for Biblical Equality, begun in the 1980s among conservative Evangelicals.

b.   C.B.E. has a strong contingent of egalitarian scholars.

4.   Vineyard Ministries   p. 128

a.   A Spirit-oriented, Biblically-based movement that has helped to facilitate the current revival is Vineyard Ministries International.

b.   Founded by John Wimber (1934-1997), this movement spread quickly among conservative Evangelicals.

N.   Conclusion   p. 129

The Early Friends truly represented the most
significant historic turning point for women
since the time of Jesus.

II.   BIBLICAL WOMANHOOD AND EARLY   Chapter 10 begins here.
       METHODISM (1739-1760)   pp. 131-144

       A.   The Methodist Revival in England (1739-   p. 131
              1760) Helped To Elevate Women.

              1.   "Emancipation of womanhood began
                     with John Wesley," says one scholar.

              2.   Methodism elevated women within a
                     more socially acceptable structure
                     than did the early Friends.

              3.   Methodism was characterized by an
                     important inclusivism of women,
                     giving them respect, recognition, and
                     freedom to minister not afforded
                     them in the state Church.

              4.   Three main elements provided this   Regarding women in
                     elevation of women.   ministry, Wesley said,
                                                              "Who am I that I should
                     a.   Wesley's central theology of   withstand God?" p. 139
                            holiness had a leveling or
                            democratizing effect not
                            present in Anglicanism.

                     b.   Welsey's mother, Susanna,
                            was a major influence.

                     c.   The Holy Spirit anointed and
                            so gifted women that Wesley
                            could not, with integrity,
                            deny their divine mandate.

       B.   The Centrality of Holiness Was a Key in   p. 138-139
              Elevating Women.

              1.   Wesley's doctrine of holiness was
                     based on Hebrews 12:14: "Pursue
                     peace with everyone, and
                     sanctification [holiness], without
                     which no one will see the Lord."

       a.   He rejected the notion that holiness was reserved for the clergy-class.

       b.   He insisted that holiness is the life-long pursuit of a lifestyle pleasing to God, enabled by the Spirit, and required by every person regardless of ecclesiastical office, social, economic or academic status, or gender.

  2.   According to Wesley, holiness held two vital requirements.   p. 139

       a.   The first was an intimate relationship with the Spirit.

       b.   The second was accountablility through public testimony of one's personal spiritual state.

C.   Susanna Annesley Wesley (1669-1742), mother of John Wesley, has been called the true founder of Methodism.   p. 132-136

  1.   As the youngest of twenty-five children, she spent much time with her Puritan father and his knowledgeable friends who debated theological issues.

  2.   While still in her teens, Susanna taught herself Hebrew, Greek, and Latin so that she could read the Bible and early Christian literature in the original languages. This enabled her to grapple with theological issues, to teach the Bible proficiently, and eventually to educate her children in things beneficial to the furtherance of the Kingdom of God.

3. She considered parental responsibility a divine mandate.

4. In defiance of cultural restrictions based on gender, she continued to minister and the parish flourished in her husband's absence.

5. What characterized Susanna's approach?

    a. She ignored the mediatoral position maintained by the Anglican church.

    b. She believed it was her personal responsibility to obey, first and foremost, the Spirit when this proved contrary to the dictates of the State church.

    c. She believed in the "present activity of the Holy Spirit" in the life of the believer.

6. Some consider Susanna to be the true founder of Methodism.   p. 136-138

D. A Large Contingent of Women Were Leaders in Early Methodism.

1. As Methodism developed under Wesley's leadership, the list of women preachers grew in number and influence, and he eventually extended preaching rights to women under his supervision.   p. 141-142

2. Mrs. Sarah Crosby's (1739-?) class attracted two hundred and the numbers alone demanded that she stand to lead and to testify.   p. 142

3. Mary Bosanquet Fletcher (1739-1815), wife of Wesley's colleague, John Fletcher, is another example of Methodism's early women leaders.   p. 142-143

IV.   CONCLUSION   p. 143

A.   Fox and the Early Friends, based on the
      revelation of the Holy Spirit confirmed by
      Holy Scripture, lived a remarkably
      egalitarian lifestyle.

B.   Wesley's inclusion of women established a
      new dignity and place hitherto denied
      women in institutional religion.

APPLICATION AND ENRICHMENT PROJECTS

1.   Locate and copy <u>Women Speaking Justified</u> by Margaret Fell.

2.   How does your Christian belief system resemble that of George Fox and how does it differ? Why?

3.   Read <u>Where Are My Susannas</u>? by Susan Hyatt.

4.   Visit the statue of Mary Dyer across from the Boston Common. Realizing that her executioners were Puritans, consider what she did and why. Does the Church today have ways of "executing" women? What can be done about it?

5.   Locate and copy pictures of some of the women in this section, such as Susanna Wesley and Margaret Fell, and frame these for your personal inspiration.

6.   Research web sites on the early Methodist women and the early Quaker women.

7.   For a real time of inspiration, read William Penn's "Preface" to George Fox' <u>Journal</u>.

8.   Read <u>The Good Fruit Remains: The Friends and Their Profound Impact</u> by Susan Hyatt on pages 79-83. (How is your personal bibliography and file coming?)

9.   Write a one-page (250-word) essay on the material in this lesson, placing emphasis on the part(s) that were most interesting or useful to you. Your paper should be double-spaced and should be typed in 12-point, Times Roman font. This will constitute page 5 of a paper that may be considered part of a final grade in this course.

FOR STUDY AND REVIEW

PART I

Based on the teaching in this lesson, indicate if the following statements are true or false by inserting a T or an F in the space provided.

1.   ___ Margaret Fell declared that opposition to women speaking comes from the spirit of darkness and apostasy that had been prevailing in the church for 1200 years.

2.   ___ Since God is no respecter of persons in that He has given each one the same potential to respond to Christ, the early Quakers believed that we are to treat all human beings with equal dignity and respect.

3.   ___ Susanna Wesley endorsed the mediatoral position of the Anglican church rather than direct and personal obedience to the indwelling Holy Spirit.

4.   ___ William Penn said of George Fox: "He exercised no authority but over evil."

5.   ___ Only men were permitted to be leaders in Methodism.

PART II

Complete the sentences by selecting the best answers from the following list:

** Mary ** Susanna Wesley ** Friends ** Margaret Fell **
** George Fox ** John Wesley **

1.   The _____, a Bible-believing, Spirit-filled revival people, were the first major advocates of biblical equality since the days of the New Testament.

2.   When George Fox met men who believed that women had no souls, "no more than a goose," he reminded them of the words of _____: "My soul doth magnify the Lord" (Lk. 1:46).

3.   In 1666, _____ wrote Women Speaking Justified, the first major book written in favor of female public ministry.

4.   _____ considered Christ the only "Head."

5.   Regarding women in ministry, _____ said, "Who am I that I should withstand God?"

6.   For various reasons, some consider _____ to have been the true founder of Methodism.

THE GOOD FRUIT REMAINS

The Friends and Their Profound Impact

By Susan C. Hyatt, D.MIN., M.A., M.A.

Some have said that a move of God must adapt to culture and human institutions if it is to have a significant and lasting impact. Is this true? Is spiritual effectiveness measured in terms of temporal structures and cultural standards? Or are God's ways, indeed, higher than human ways? And are we willing to trust God enough to do things His way?

One example of the power of being Spirit-led rather than being institutionally oriented is the early Quaker Movement, or the Society of Friends (Jn. 15:15), as they preferred to be called. They came into view in England about 1650 and in one generation became the fastest growing movement in the Western world with 40-60,000 adherents by 1660. In only 40 years, Friends spread the Gospel from Turkey to the English Colonies in the New World.

The Friends were charismatic believers, the spiritual gifts being common in their midst. They experienced miracles and practiced singing in the Spirit. Edward Burroughs writes, "Our tongues were loosed and our mouths opened, and we spake with new tongues, as the Lord gave utterance."

Quakerism arose in England during a period when English society was in tremendous flux. The old, medieval culture was disintegrating and the struggle to find a new locus of authority and control was the paramount issue. As England swayed between Romanism and Protestantism, the Act of Supremacy of 1534 declared the king "the supreme head of the church of England," and the Stuarts held to the "divine right of kings," that is,

the alleged, God-ordained right to ultimate authority. In addition, the Reformers (1517-1648) had made the scriptures a "paper pope," essentially transferring authority to their interpretation of scripture. In contrast to all of this, the Friends claimed the authority of the indwelling Holy Spirit who had given the scriptures.

TWO KEY LEADERS

The primary shapers of the Society of Friends were George Fox (1624-91) and Margaret Fell (1614-1702).

GEORGE FOX

George Fox had little education but, having been reared in a strict Puritan-Presbyterian home, he possessed an intense love for and a thorough knowledge of the Bible. His voluminous writings reflect his remarkable biblical literacy. His associates used to say, "Though the Bible were lost, it might be found in the mouth of George Fox."

Fox's intense hunger for a vital relationship with God was satisfied when he heard a voice say to him, "There is one, even Christ Jesus, that can speak to thy condition." He writes, "When I heard it, my heart did leap for joy . . . and I knew [God] experimentally." He began urging his listeners to renounce "self-performance" to heed the leading of "the light of Christ within."

Because Fox was admired by so many, some accused him of seeking control over others. But, says his associate, Wm. Penn, "He exercised no authority but over evil."

MARGARET ASKEW FELL

Margaret Fell, an Anglican gentry, wife of Judge Fell, and mother of eight, was converted when she heard Fox explain the Gospel. The Fell estate, Swarthmoor Hall, immediately became a vital center of Quaker activity. Margaret Fell was instrumental in stabilizing the Women's Meetings which helped women learn to exercise their equality in the Society.

She wrote and published voluminously, a fact that gave her high visibility and recognition. While in prison in 1666, she wrote Women Speaking Justified, the first book by a woman promoting female public ministry. Fell was among the first of the Quaker leaders to correspond with the Jewish leader Menassah Ben Israel and other Jews of Holland regarding Jewish reentry to England. Her tracts were translated into Latin, Dutch, and Hebrew.

THE KEY PRINCIPLE

THE INNER LIGHT

It has been said that Quakerism is a lifestyle as opposed to a doctrinal system. The definitive principle of this lifestyle is the Inner Light found in various passages and clearly stated in John 1:1-9. Fox believed that "'there was that of God,' . . . in all men and women everywhere." This is the key to Fox. It gave him confidence in evangelism, for it meant that the potential to respond to the Gospel was inherent in every person. It also gave him an egalitarian world view for it indicated that God was no respecter of persons. According to William Penn's "Preface" to Fox's Journal, this Inner Light give awareness of sin, of the spirit of the world, and of the fallen nature of humanity. It conjures a genuine sorrow for sin, revealing not only the awful nature of sin but also the saving work of Jesus Christ on the Cross. It alerts the redeemed to walk in holiness of thought, word, and deed, and in love of God and others.

IMPLICATIONS

William Penn delineates 1a number of implications of the Inner Light. The goal of these principles, he explains, is "to bring things back into their primitive and right order again." Briefly stated, they are:

- To commune with and love one another.

- To love enemies, taking no revenge, but forgiving.

- To speak the truth at all times and obey the prohibition regarding oaths (Mt. 5).

- To use energy to fight sin and Satan, not people, and to be willing to suffer if necessary.

- To refuse to pay tithes but instead to follow Christ's command: "Freely you have received, freely give."

- To treat all people with equal respect, not using flattering titles nor vain gestures and compliments.

- To use plain language in addressing all people so as not to elevate one person above another by means of titles.

- To value silence and solitude, but when in company to be careful to keep discussion brief and profitable.

- Neither to drink to people nor to pledge by oath-taking.

- To make marriage coincide with the biblical mandate of equal meet-helps.

- To avoid pomp, ceremonies, and festivals in relation to births and naming children.

- To keep burials simple and to avoid outward symbols of mourning in dress and ceremony.

CONSEQUENCE & INFLUENCE

The impact of the Quaker lifestyle was revolutionary and intense. The idea that God would take up residence in each person meant that each person could gain a new sense of his or her personal worth in the sight of God. By the same token, it required equal respect for all people because the same Christ dwelt in each one. The actual experience of knowing Christ intimately gave believers new confidence. But this inner connection threatened the ability of the institutional church—which depended on outward symbols of authority, such as the priesthood, clerical robes, church buildings, and sacraments—to control the masses.

PERSECUTION

Persecution was severe. At one time, 15,000 Friends were in English prison and 450 died there. In New England, persecution from the Puritans reached savage heights. Much of this arose because of the Quaker threat to the Puritan patriarchal structures and a theocracy that continued to combine the authority of church and state. The possibility of women preachers was most alarming, and consequently, anti-Quaker propaganda published in Boston linked Quakerism to witchcraft. Mary Fisher and Ann Austin, the first Quaker missionaries to Boston, arrived on July 11, 1656, and were immediately denounced as heretics and unsubmissive women. They were stripped naked, searched for signs of witchcraft, and isolated for 5 weeks in prison before being extradited. When Mary Dyer visited Boston in 1659 to comfort imprisoned Quakers, she was sentenced to death ad, to the beating of a drum, was led through the streets to the gallows. Already bound and noosed for execution, she was suddenly released. In the spring of 1660, however, feeling she could not accept this stay of execution, she returned to Boston, where, this time, the Puritan authorities hanged her. Her statue stands on the grounds of the Boston State House, a symbol of freedom of conscience.

INFLUENCE

Despite persecution, the Friends flourished, especially during the formative colonial period in America. They were trailblazers in a number of important areas and their legacy remains strong today.

1. **The Abolition Movement.** Quakers were champions of abolition of the slaves. In 1657, Fox had written a letter denouncing the captivity of Black and Indian slaves. The Friends were actually the first to make a direct assault against slavery. Sixty years before the Emancipation Proclamation, there was not one Quaker slave-holder in America. In the mid-19th century, they conducted the underground railroad providing for the safe conduct of escaped and freed slaves to the Canadian border.

2. **Prison Reform.** Quaker women had been active in prison reform ever since 1655 when Elizabeth Hooten wrote a letter to the English king protesting prison conditions. Elizabeth Guerney Fry (1780-1845), an English Quaker preacher, is commonly acknowledged as the founder of prison reform. In America in 1787, Quakers in Philadelphia organized the Society for Alleviating the Miseries of the Public Prisons. Their first effort was "to convert the Walnut Street prison into a penitentiary, a place where prisoners had the opportunity to meditate upon their sins and repent, while being given moral instruction by a groups of visitors."

3. **Indian Affairs.** In America, Quakers were trusted by the Indians. Knowing the Pennsylvania Quakers were their friends, they asked them to represent their interests

when they made treaties with the new American government. In 1794, 4 Quakers went to Canandaigua, New York, to protect the interests of the Six nations in the treaty signing with the United States. Various yearly committees established centers on reservatons to teach farming and other helpful skills to Indians.

4. Government Policy. William Penn (1644-1718) played a key tole in American colonization. In 1682, he and 11 other Friends bought northern New Jersey, and later he received the grant of Pennsylvania from the British Crown. Penn also helped lay the foundation for the pattern of US government by suggestions he presented to the Royal Commission in 1697. He suggested a union of the colonies, and he helped plan for the Senate 100 years in advance by proposing an elected congress composed of 2 representatives from each colony.

5. Co-Education. George Fox insisted on the revolutionary idea of equal education for boys and girls. He recommended the founding of a school in Shacklewell, England, "for instructing girls and young maidens in whatsoever things are civil and useful in the creation." A number of prestigious educational institutions have resulted from this perspective.

FURTHER INFLUENCE

In addition to these influences, various important movements have been seeded by Quakerism. Indeed, 3 movements—the Women's Suffrage Movement, early Pentecostalism, and Christians for Biblical Equality—are of Quaker heritage. These 3 movements point to the dynamic egalitarianism generated by Quaker founders George Fox and Margaret Fell. This originated in their devotion to the Lord Jesus Christ, to the indwelling Spirit, and to their interpretation of scripture.

1. Women Suffrage Movement. The Women's Suffrage Movement gained corporate identity at Seneca Falls, New York at a meeting in the Wesleyan Chapel, July 19-20, 1848 through the efforts of four Quaker women and one Quaker sympathizer. Formulated by these Friends, their Declaration of Sentiments putting forth a statement of equal rights for women. This statement was ratified by 68 women and 32 men. Quaker women nurtured the fledgling movement, and the long fight for the vote for women was led by Quaker women: Lucretia Mott (1793-1880), Elizabeth Cady Stanton (1815-1902), Susan B. Anthony (1820-1906), and Alice Paul. The suffrage bill (June 1919) and the 19th Amendment to the Constitution (August 26, 1920) were the fruit of their faith and labors.

2. Early Pentecostalism. Quaker influence was also significantly present in the early Pentecostal Revival (1901-06). The initial outpouring occurred at the 1900 Watch Night Service of Bethel Bible School in Topeka, Kansas, a Bible school operated by Charles Parham, Sarah Thistlethwaite-Parham, and Lilian Thislethwaite. Although Bethel is commonly considered a Holiness school, it should be remembered that the Thislethwaite sisters were birthright Friends and that Parham himself had spent many hours modifying his Methodist theology in dialogue with his wife's Quaker grandfather, David Baker, in Tonganoxie, Kansas. While the Parham-Thislethwaite influence prevailed (1900-06), a gender and racial equality and a Quaker dignity characterized the Revival. (Indeed, Parham was hardly a racist, as current misinformation charges!) This was the case in the their revivals in Tri-State area of Kansas-Oklahoma-Missouri; in South Texas; in Zion City, Illinois; and from these regional revivals thousands of men and women carried the message around the world. As the revival spread beyond the Parham-Thislethwaite influence—at Azusa Street, among the Southern Holiness groups, and among Baptistic and Reformed people—hierarchicalism pushed out egalitarianism, and other Quaker characteristics gave way to cultural and denominational practices.

3. <u>Christians for Biblical Equality</u>. A third movement with a Quaker connection is Christians for Biblical Equality, begun in the 1980s among conservative Evangelicals. Chief catalyst and organizer of C.B.E. Catherine Clark Kroeger. Dr. Kroeger did her undergraduate studies at Bryn Mawr College, a prestigious Friends' women's college. C.B.E. boasts a strong contingent of egalitarian scholars, and is gaining influence through local chapters, conventions, and publications including periodicals. <u>The Priscilla Papers</u>, one of the periodicals, was also the name of the periodical published by women in the evangelical wing of Quakerism about this the time C.B.E. started. Having developed great interest in Quaker women's history, these women formed a Task Force on Women and helped expose Quakers to their egalitarian heritage.

REFLECTIONS

The fastest growing segment of Christendom today, the Pentecostal/Charismatic community, stands only to gain from an informed examination of the lifestyle of the early Friends. At stake, ultimately, is the age-old issue of authority. The early Friends demonstrated how authority is to remain with God and is expressed by His Spirit and through his Word. People of faith have responsibility, not authority, to interpret correctly the Word of truth and to be worthy ambassadors in the earth.

If we need further evidence of the impact of the early Friends, consider that Voltaire, the renowned atheist, called the Quakers of his day "the most truly Christian of people." "By their fruit you shall know them," said Jesus.

(This article is taken from an extensive, unpublished manuscript by Susan Hyatt and appeared in the <u>Hyatt Quarterly</u>, Summer 1997. Also, references to the quotations can be found in the textbook in Chapter 9, pp. 83-130.)

LESSON 6

Spirit-Led Advances for Women in 19th Century America, Part I

LESSON 6

Spirit-Led Advances for Women in 19th C. America – Part I

❑ THEME: The Holy Spirit continued to build on the theological foundation of the Friends and Methodists; and women, motivated by the Spirit, continued to advance toward equality in 19th Century America.

❑ PURPOSE: To show the continuing advance toward equality for women, prompted by the activity of the Spirit among Bible-believing men and, especially, women.

❑ OBJECTIVES:

    1.   To showcase some of the Christian women who made a difference.

    2.   To get a sense of the Christian commitment driving these women.

❑ TEXTBOOK READING: Chapter 11, pp. 145-176 only.

❑ SUGGESTED READING AND TEACHER RESOURCES:

    • Booth, Catherine. Female Ministry. Reprint of the First Ed., 1859. New York: Salvation Army Printing & Publishing Dept., 1975.

    • Bushnell, Katherine. God's Word to Women. Mossville, IL: God's Word to Women Publishers, Reprint. N.d.

    • Collect as many pictures as possible of the women showcased in this lesson.

    • Collect as many of their books as possible to show to the students.

    • Do "web work" related to the teaching.

    • Hardwick, Dana. Thou That Bringest Good Tidings: The Life and Work of Katharine C. Bushnell. Minneapolis: Christian for Biblical Equality, 1995.

    • Raser, Harold E. Phoebe Palmer: Her Life and Thought. Lewiston, NY: Edwin Mellen Press, 1987.

    • Smith, Hannah Whitall. The Christian's Secret to a Happy Life. 19th Printing. Old Tappan: Spire, 1975.

❏   LECTURE OUTLINE: QUESTIONS, NOTES, AND
                                                        TEXTBOOK REFERENCES

I.   INTRODUCTION: p. 145-146

       Nineteenth-century America saw a convergence of
       elements that elevated women. Motivated by the
       Holy Spirit, these elements loosened—and in some
       cases, broke—the cultural restraints that had
       chained women for centuries. They can be divided
       into two main historical categories: pre-Civil War
       (to about 1860), and post Civil War (after 1865).

       A.   Pre-Civil War Events that Elevated Women   p. 146

              1.   The Quakers remained a force in
                     American culture and continued, at
                     least to some extent, to stand for
                     women and equality in a way that
                     other groups did not.

              2.   Methodism, with its inclusivism of
                     women, had come to America in
                     1760 where it had become the
                     nation's largest denomination.

              3.   The revivalism of Charles Finney   p. 146-148
                     (1792-1875) and Asa Mahan (1799-
                     1889), had brought social reforms
                     that included the elevation of
                     women.

                     a.   The most controversial of   p. 147
                            Finney's "new measures"
                            during the Second Great   Note: Mahan's suggested
                            Awakening (1800-1840) was   tombstone epitaph:
                            his practice of allowing   The first man, in the
                            women to pray aloud and   history of the race, who
                            testify in mixed gatherings.   conducted women, in
                                                           connection with members
                     b.   Finney and Mahan helped   of the opposite sex,
                            establish Oberlin College   through a full course of
                            (1833), the first   liberal education, and
                            coeducational college in the   conferred upon her the
                            world, for the purpose of   high degrees which had
                            perpetuating Finney's "blend   hitherto been exclusive
                            of revivalism and reform."   prerogative of men (148).

4.   America's special sense of divine   pp. 148-150
        destiny helped produce a social
        conscience that called for an end to
        social sins, especially slavery.

        a.   This trend progressed
                through the Abolition
                Movement and culminated in
                the Civil War (1861-65).

        b.   Angelina (1792-1873) and   p. 147
                Sarah (1805-1879) Grimké
                shook New England in the
                1830s by public anti-slavery
                activism which included
                lecturing and writing.

        c.   This public display by
                women shocked the
                Calvinist-Puritan status quo
                which upheld the idea of
                strictly predestined social
                roles based on gender and
                color. In this way of
                thinking, both women and
                people of color were to be
                silent and to serve.

5.   In the advance toward abolition, the   p. 149
        proof-texting approach to biblical
        interpretation was replaced by so-
        called "abolitionist hermeneutic."

        a.   This method embraced broad
                scriptural principles.

        b.   It set passages in their
                legitimate contexts.

        c.   Its theological starting point
                was Galatians 3:28.

7.   The American Civil War (1861-65)   p. 149
        together with the Spirit-driven social
        changes that were in motion helped
        break the back of hyper-Calvinism in
        America.

8.   The victory was important to women for a number of reasons.   pp. 149-150

   a.   It brought women into the public arena.

   b.   It strengthened the public speaking skills of those women who were bold enough to preach, speak, and debate on behalf of the slaves.

   c.   It challenged the idea of predestined roles based on skin color, thereby opening the possibility that God did not, in fact, have predestined social roles dictated by skin color or gender.

   d.   It called forth an approach to biblical interpretation that led to a more accurate reading of the text which helped advance the biblical truth of women's equality.

B.   Post-Civil War Events that Elevated Women   p. 150

Following this war, important movements, interwoven in many cases, arose and contributed to a further loosening of restraints on women and a trend toward gender equality. These movements were:

1.   The Holiness Movement

2.   Women's Christian Temperance Movement

3.   The Missionary Movement

4.   The Women's Suffrage Movement

5.   The Healing Movement

6.   The Quaker women revived

II.   THE HOLINESS MOVEMENT   p. 150-151

    A.   What Was the Holiness Movement?

        1.   It was an attempt, begun among Methodists, to experience the spiritual dynamism first-generation Methodism, and it eventually spread to affect every denomination in America.

        2.   A return to Wesley's ideas of a life-changing experience subsequent to conversion and the accompanying need to testify publicly to one's spiritual state brought renewal, mostly through meetings in homes, a milieu that gave women a greater opportunity to participate.

        3.   So vital was this approach that it produced a state of Christian influence throughout the nation, even among non-Methodists, known as the Holiness Movement.

    B.   Biblical Themes for Equality Arose in the Holiness Movement.

        1.   The Galatians 3:28 Theme of Biblical Equality   p. 151

            a.   This became the battle cry for the liberation of women.   p. 151-154

            b.   In 1891, Wm. B. Godbey wrote, "It is the God-given right, blood-bought privilege, and bounden duty of the women, as well as the men, to preach the gospel."   Consider reading aloud some of the inspiring quotations.

            c.   B. T. Roberts (1823-1893), founder of the Free Methodist Church (1860), debated in favor of both an egalitarian marriage relationship and the ordination of women.

    d.   <u>Review of the Churches</u>, (Feb.-April 1892) reports comments by Josephine Butler, Mrs. Sheldon Amos, and Mrs. Bramwell Booth in their article, "Woman's Place in the Church."   p. 152. Read the quotation.

  2. The Redemption Argument for Biblical Equality.   p. 154

    a.   The point is this: If woman was, indeed, under a curse through the fall, now, by virtue of redemption, the curse associated with that event has been broken by the work of the Jesus Christ.

    b.   Seth Cook Rees declares, "As the grace of God and the light of the Gospel are shed abroad . . . woman is elevated, until at Pentecost she stands, a second Eve, by the side of her husband."

  3. The Pentecostal Theme for Biblical Equality.   p. 155

Based on Joel 2:28 and Acts 2:17-18, this argument points to the equal outpouring of the Spirit on men and women alike, empowering both equally for End-Time ministry.

C. The Leading Minister of the Holiness Movement was Phoebe Palmer.   p. 155-164

  1. Phoebe Palmer

    a.   Phoebe Worrall Palmer (1807-1874) grew up in a devout Methodist home in New York City, and as a

<table>
<tr><td colspan="2">young person was consumed with a hunger to know God.</td><td></td></tr>
</table>

b.	Phoebe married Dr. Walter Clarke Palmer (1804-1883), a prominent New York physician who shared Phoebe's consuming passion to serve the Lord.	pp, 156, 158 Show their picture.
3.	Obedience to God's call resulted in Phoebe's becoming one of the most influential leaders of the Holiness Movement.	p. 156
a.	She was its dominant theologian	p. 156-160, esp. 160.
b.	She was the foremost Bible teacher.	Show her books:
c.	She was a prominent evangelist.	• The Way of Holiness (1843)
d.	She was its most influential writer.	• The Pomise of the Father (1859)
e.	She made tremendous impact as editor of the major Holiness periodical The Guide to Holiness (1864-74).	• Four Years in the Old World (1867) p. 164
f.	She was a founder of prestigious Drew University (1866/1868) in Madison, New Jersey.	
g.	One of her books, the 421-page The Promise of the Father (1859), articulates a biblical theology validating woman's right and responsibility to obey the call to public ministry.	pp. 161-163
3.	Phoebe endured criticism and ridicule as a woman in ministry.	p. 161
4.	Searching remarks such as the following from The Promise of the Father, never leave us:	p. 164

The church in many ways is a sort of potter's field, where the gifts of woman, as so many strangers, are buried. How long, O Lord, how long before man shall roll away the stone that we may see a resurrection?

Daughters of Zion, from the dust
Exalt thy fallen head;
Again in thy Redeemer trust.—
He calls thee from the dead.

D.   Hundreds of Holiness Women Left Their Mark on the Church and on Society.

    1.   Alma White (1862-1946) founded the Pillar of Fire Church.

p. 164

    2.   Catherine Mumford Booth (1829-1890) was "an unfailing, unflinching, uncompromising champion of woman's rights."

p. 165
Show her book: Female Ministry.

        a.   Co-founder of the Salvation Army with her husband, Wm. Booth (1829-1912), she worked tirelessly for equal authority, equal rights, and equal responsibilities for women on the basis of redemption and Pentecost.

        b.   In the marriage relationship, she staunchly refused to be considered or treated anything but equal with her husband.

        c.   She wrote her a thirty-two page tract entitled Female Ministry in which she laments the inequality of women as "a remarkable device of the devil," but she triumphantly proclaims, "the time of her deliverance draweth nigh."

3.   Mrs. Amanda Matthews-Berry Smith (1837-1915) began preaching in 1870 and continued with tremendous success despite cruel racism and barbarous sexism.

p. 165

4.   Mrs. Jenny Fowler Willing, a contributing editor of <u>The Guide to Holiness</u> in the 1890s, was a relentless advocate of biblical equality.

p. 166-167

Read quotation on marriage, p. 167.

She charges that woman is inclined to be content "with shining, like the moon, with borrowed splendor, as the mother, sister, or wife of the great so-and-so. . . . She has left her talent in its napkin while she has been obeying the world's dictum by helping make the most of his."

p. 166

III.   THE HOLINESS MOVEMENT AND QUAKER WOMEN.

p. 167

Read B. T. Roberts quote on pp. 167-168.

A.   Especially after 1860, through the Holiness Revival, the Holy Spirit reawakened Quaker women.

B.   Female subjugation was intolerable among the Quakers.

The quotes on pp. 168-171 are intensely motivational, showing the deep commitment of these women of God.

C.   The influence of powerful, Spirit-motivated, Quaker women in advancing social reform in the latter half of the 1800s is enormous.

D.   Hannah Whitall Smith (1832-1911) is, perhaps, the most widely known of the Quaker women among conservative Christians today.

p. 171

1.   Her classic book <u>The Christian's Secret of a Happy Life</u>, first published in 1875, is still available.

Show copy of <u>The Christian's Secret of a Happy Life</u>. By 1975, over 2 million copies had been sold.

2.   She and her husband, Robert Pearsall Smith, were active in the Keswick "deeper life" movement in England.

3.   Hannah was deeply involved in movements with special concerns for the welfare and equality of women.

IV.   THE CHRISTIAN WOMEN'S TEMPERANCE MOVEMENT

A.   The Women's Crusade of 1873-74.   p. 172

1.   In Ohio and New York, women banned together protesting the sale of liquor in an all-out effort to halt the suffering of women and children brought on by drunken husbands.

2.   In fifty days, the women halted the liquor traffic in "two hundred and fifty towns, increased by one hundred percent the attendance at church and decreased that at the criminal courts in like proportion."

B.   The National Woman's Christian Temperance Union (WCTU) Grew out of the Crusades in 1874.   pp. 172-174

1.   It was a Christian women's movement for "the protection of the home."   p. 173

2.   It happened outside the jurisdiction of the institutional Church.   p. 175

Frances Willard said, this was so, "not because they wish to be so," but because the church "is afraid of her own gentle, earnest -hearted daughters."   Show picture of Frances Willard, and a copy of her biography, <u>The Beautiful Life of Francis Willard</u>.

3.   The work of WCTU was extensive, going far beyond supporting biblical values for women and children.   p. 174-175.

4.   The WCTU, through the work of Frances Willard, became the largest woman's organization in the world with works in 50 nations.   p. 173

C.   Frances Willard. (1839-98) was WCTU's president from 1879 until 1898

     1.   She and Hannah Whitall Smith were close friends, and Hannah became the first superintendent of the Evangelistic Department.   p. 173

     2.   As with the other women in the movement, Willard drew strength and direction from her relationship with God.

         a.   She had grown up on Finney revivalism.   p. 173

         b.   She experienced sanctification at Phoebe Palmer's meetings.   p. 173

         c.   Her deep dependence on the Lord is obvious in her description of her divine call to become active in the suffrage movement.   p. 173-174. Read the quotation.

         d.   Willard credits her vision and organizational ability to the Lord: "[Only] as I come close to God and through Christ's blood am made a new creature, am I ready for this work so blessed and so high."   p. 174

D.   Dr. Katherine C. Bushnell (1855-1946) has become increasingly well known for her book God's Word to Women.   p. 175.

Show her book God's Word to Women.

Also show her biography Thou That Bringest God Tidings.

     1.   After a time as a Methodist Episcopal medical missionary in China, she had a medical practice in Denver.

     2.   Frances Willard persuaded her to become the National Evangelist of the WCTU's Department for the Advancement of Social Purity.   p. 175

3.   Bushnell's final crusade came through the power of the pen.   p. 176

While a doctor in China, she had begun to see how culturally-biased translations of the Bible intensified female bondage. Because she knew that the true Gospel heals and liberates, she devoted the last forty years of her life in diligent language study, biblical translation, and writing. Among her voluminous writings is the Bible study, God's Word to Women.

5.   Biographer Dana Hardwick notes that Bushnell "saw the task of educated women as twofold."

     a.   She believed, "They must spread to all women in all places the full gospel message of the same freedom and equality as men have in Jesus Christ."   p. 176

     b.   And she believed, "Educated women must attack the 'false teachings as to the place of women in God's economy' and break . . . the 'tyranny'" of biased, erroneous biblical translation and commentaries."   p. 176

V.   CONCLUSION

A.   Women Had Made Significant Advances.

B.   The Motivation for This Came from a Deep Commitment to the Lord.

C.   The Energy of These Women Went to Helping Relieve the Distress of Others, not Toward Building Kingdoms for Themselves.

APPLICATION AND ENRICHMENT PROJECTS

1.   Web Work: Do a search of topics such as abolition, the Grimké Sisters, WCTU, and other key topics in this lesson.

2.   If you have not done so, read Where Are My Susannas? by Susan Hyatt.

3.   Locate in books or on the web, pictures of the women studied in this lesson; for example: Catherine Booth, Alma White, Amanda Smith, Hannah Whitall Smith, Francis Willard, Phoebe Palmer, Katherine Bushnell, and others. Frame them and let them be a constant inspiration or reminder.

4.   Go through this lesson and list the books by these women. Do your best to obtain copies.

5.   Read Dana Hardwick's biography of Katherine Bushnell, Thou That Bringest Good Tidings. It is available from Christian for Biblical Equality.

6.   Visit the web site: http://www.godswordtowomen.org.

7.   Read Catherine Booth's book, Female Ministry. For copies, contact the Salvation Army Printing and Publishing Department, 145 West 15th Street, New York, New York 10011.

8.   What is your opinion of the women in this lesson? Do you think that, generally speaking, Christian women today have the exhibit the courage and motivation that they displayed? Why? Why not?

9.   Visit the Phoebe Palmer Collection in the Archives at Drew University in Madison, New Jersey.

10.   Write a one-page (250-word) essay on the material in this lesson, placing emphasis on the part(s) that were most interesting or useful to you. Your paper should be double-spaced and should be typed in 12-point, Times Roman font. This will constitute page 6 of a paper that may be considered part of a final grade in this course.

FOR STUDY AND REVIEW

PART I

Based on the teaching in this lesson, indicate if the following statements are true or false by inserting a T or an F in the space provided.

1. ____ Nineteenth-century America saw a convergence of Spirit-motivated movements that elevated women toward equality.

2. ____ Catherine Booth said that the equality of women is "a remarkable device of the devil."

3. ____ The WCTU, a Christian women's movement for "the protection of the home," became the largest woman's organization in the world with works in 50 nations.

4. ____ Katherine Bushnell believed that educated women should remain silent and submitted to the "biased and erroneous biblical translations and commentaries."

5. ____ At least 3 Biblical themes promoting equality arose in the Holiness Movement: the Galatians 3:28 theme, the Redemption theme, and the Pentecostal theme.

PART II

Complete the sentences by selecting the best answers from the following list:

** Katherine Bushnell ** Catherine Booth ** Phoebe Palmer **
** Hannah Whitall Smith ** Frances Willard **

1. Obedience to the call of God by _____ resulted in her becoming the most influential leader of the Holiness Movement.

2. _____, cofounder of the Salvation Army, was "an unfailing, unflinching, uncompromising champion of woman's rights" who staunchly refused to be considered or treated anything but equal with her husband.

3. _____, a Quaker who wrote the classic book The Christian's Secret of a Happy Life, was deeply involved in movements with special concerns for the welfare and equality of women in society and in marriage.

4. The founder of the Woman's Christian Temperance Union, _____, drew strength and direction from her personal relationship with the Lord.

5. _____ wrote the classic book God's Word to Women.

LESSON 7

Spirit-Led Advances for Women
in 19th Century America, Part II

LESSON 7

Spirit-Led Advances for Women in 19th C. America – Part II

☐ THEME: On the American scene, in particular, the Holy Spirit continued to build on the foundation of the Friends and Methodists, and women, motivated by the Spirit, made unprecedented strides ahead in 19th Century America.

☐ PURPOSE: To show the continuing advance toward biblically-based equality for women, prompted by the activity of the Spirit in a Christian-oriented culture.

☐ OBJECTIVES:

    1.   To continue to showcase some of the Christian women in their advance toward biblically-based, Spirit-motivated equality.

    2.   To trace that activity to the early Pentecostal Revival (1901-05).

☐ TEXTBOOK READING: Pages 145-206

☐ SUGGESTED READING AND TEACHER RESOURCES:

- Procure a USA Susan B. Anthony silver dollar. These are usually available as change in post office stamp machines.

- Gordon, Anna A. The Beautiful Life of Frances Willard. Chicago: Woman's Temperance Publishing Association, 1898.

- Make a copy of the Declaration of Sentiments (1848) written by Quaker women and used as a basis for the suffrage movement. http://www.luminet.net/~tgort/convent.htm, pp. 3-7.

- Parham, Sarah. The Life of Charles Fox Parham. Joplin: Tri-State Printing, 1930.

- Stevens, Doris. Jailed for Freedom: American Women Win the Vote. Ed. Carol O'Hare from the 1920 Ed.. Troutdale, OR: NewSage Press, 1996.

- Tucker, Ruth A,. and Walter Liefeld, Daughters of the Church: Women and Ministry from New Testament Times to the Present. Grand Rapids: Zondervan, 1987.

- Woodworth-Etter, Maria. Signs and Wonders. Tulsa: Harrison House, 1980.

❑ LECTURE OUTLINE:

I.   INTRODUCTION

Briefly review Lesson 6, but only if necessary.

II.   SPIRIT-LED WOMEN FIGHT FOR FREEDOM TO VOTE

This was Spirit-motivated, Quaker women who led the 70-year-long suffrage movement giving American women the right to vote.

A.   Susan B. Anthony (1820-1906).

    1.   Along with Elizabeth Cady Stanton, she founded the National Woman Suffrage Association (1870).

    2.   Anthony was a colleague of Hannah Whitall Smith and Frances Willard and had been an ardent abolitionist.

    3.   She is best remembered, however, for her persistent, pioneering efforts that culminated in women in the United States gaining the right to vote in 1920. She writes:

I do pray, and that most earnestly and constantly, for some terrific shock to startle women of the nation into a self-respect which will compel them to see the absolute degradation of their present position; which will compel them to break their yoke of bondage and give them faith in themselves; which will make them proclaim their allegiance to women first . . .. The fact is, women are in chains, and their servitude is all the more debasing because they do not realize it. Oh to compel them to see and tell and to give them courage and the conscience to speak and act for their own freedom, though they face the scorn and contempt of all the world for doing it!

QUESTIONS, NOTES, AND TEXTBOOK REFERENCES

p. 176.

Key here is "Spirit-led."

Why are we not taught this in the Church?

Pass around a Susan B. Anthony Silver Dollar. Why have we not been told of her Christian motivation and character?

p. 177.

B.   Hannah Whitall Smith, too, crusaded for equality for women.

1.   She was convinced that suffrage was a Christian cause, and in describing a speech she made on suffrage, she said,

In my speech I said I had come to the advocacy of this reform by the way of the gospel, that Christ came to break every yoke and set free all that were bound, and that I wanted to follow in his steps and share in his work. I said the gospel did not arbitrarily upset the existing order of things, but it put a mine under all wrong and oppression that finally blew it up. And that therefore women were made free by the working out of the principles of Christ who had declared there is neither male nor female in him.

p. 177

2.   Smith was also an advocate of biblical equality in marriage. To her daughter, she wrote:

I am thoroughly roused on the subject for I have had so many cases of grievous oppression of men over their wives lately that my blood boils with indignation. And before thee is married I want to have thy position as an equal with thy husband settled on a legal basis. The moment one looks into the subject at all it seems utterly incomprehensible how we women could have endured it as patiently has we have. Literally and truly up to within a very few years women have been simply *slaves*. And some women say they like it! Ugh! Nothing but the vote will set us at liberty but that will, for then we shall be not only women, but *human* beings as well. Now we are nothing but women.

p. 178

C.   The Declaration of Sentiments was written by Quaker women.

    1.   The Suffrage Movement gained corporate identity at Seneca Falls, New York on July 19-20, 1848 through the leadership efforts of four Quaker women Lucretia Coffin Mott, Martha Coffin Wright, Jane Hunt, Mary Ann McClintock, and a Quaker sympathizer, Elizabeth Cady Stanton.

    2.   Some see this event as the birth of feminism, and perhaps they are correct. Regardless, it should benoted that this movement was born in the hearts of Spirit-oriented, Bible-believing women. These women faced persecution, incarceration, suffering, and defamation not unlike that of their seventeenth-century Quaker ancestors.

D.   Quaker Women Devoted Their Entire Lives to Win the Long and Very Difficult Fight for Woman's Right to Vote.

    1.   Like the early Quaker women, they often found themselves persecuted and jailed, but driven by a sense of what was right and motivated by the Spirit of God, they did not cease.

    2.   Susan B. Anthony's successor was Quaker, Alice Paul (1885-1977).

        a.   She was at the helm when Congress passed the women's suffrage bill in June, 1919.

        b.   The 19th Amendment to the Constitution became law on August 26, 1920, giving women the right to vote.

---

pp. 178-179

Make copies and distribute, if possible.

Why has the Church not championed these women, but instead, has let the world exalt them as their heroines?

This meeting was conducted in the Wesleyan Chapel.

In some of the denominations, women were not given the vote in church-related business until the 1990s.

p. 179-80

III.   WOMEN IN THE MISSIONARY MOVEMENT   p. 180

    A.   The Missionary Movement of the late
        nineteenth century opened new opportunities
        for meaningful ministry for women.

        1.   This endeavor was "substantially   p. 180
            larger than any of the other mass
            women's movements in the
            nineteenth century."

        2.   Both married and single women
            went abroad as "sent ones," while at
            home, thousands of women banned
            together in support of their sisters'
            missionary endeavors.

    B.   Women's Missionary Societies Emerged   p. 180-182
        Apart from the Churches.

        1.   By 1861, Christian women had   p. 181
            developed sufficient autonomy and
            strength to operate the
            interdenominational Woman's Union
            Missionary Society of America.

        2.   Women's missionary societies raised   p. 181
            large sums of money, provided the
            first missionary literature, held
            missionary conventions and
            institutes, sent and supported single
            women missionaries and rendered
            critical support to wives of
            missionary husbands

    C.   Women Paid a High Price.   p. 182-183

        1.   Missionary women of this era were
            outstanding pioneers and heroes of
            the faith; for example, Mary Slessor,
            Amy Carmichael, and Lottie Moon.

        2.   The lot of married women in
            missions was especially trying.

        3.   Ann Hassletine Judson, wife of
            Adoniram Judson, used writing

successfully as a tool to educate readers at home

D.   Reaching Women, the Priority.   p. 183-184

    1.   Many women began to recognize that the single most important missionary endeavor was to reach the mothers.

    2.   By 1894, thirty-three women's foreign mission boards had sponsored about one thousand women as teachers, doctors, evangelists, and relief workers.

    3.   This development brought censor in 1888 from the Baptist leaders who warned women "to recognize the leadership of men . . . so as not to discredit the natural and predestined headship of man in Missions."

IV.   WOMEN WERE PROMINENT IN THE HEALING MOVEMENT.   p. 184

A.   Women in the Early Days of the Healing Movement.

    1.   Mother Anna Lee (1736-81),   p. 185
        founded the Shakers.

    2.   Ellen Gould White (1827-1915)   p. 185
        founded the Adventists in 1840, a group who prayed for the sick based on biblical precedents.

    3.   Mrs. Elizabeth Mix, a well-educated   p. 185
        woman from Wolcottville, Connecticut, was healed of tuberculosis through the ministry of Ethan O. Allen.

B.   Faith Homes and Women.   p. 186

    1.   By 1887, the practice of divine healing and the concept of the faith

home had become so popular, especially in America, that more than thirty such centers were in operation.

2.   The practice of divine healing and the concept of faith homes merged with the Holiness Movement so that many of the healing homes were operated by Holiness women.

p. 186

C.   Ministers of Divine Healing.

p. 187

1.   Dr. Charles Cullis, the single, most important figure in the Healing Movement, received his sanctification experience in 1862 through Phoebe Palmer's ministry.

3.   Dr. A. J. Gordon (1836-95), a Boston pastor of great intellectual and spiritual stature was an ardent Holiness advocate and supporter of divine healing.

p. 187

a.   Gordon and his Clarendon Street Church were on the forefront of important social action including world missions, temperance, and women's rights.

b.   His 1894 work, The Ministry of Women, remains an important statement of support for women.

4.   A. B. Simpson (1843-1919), a Presbyterian pastor and Holiness leader, founded the Christian and Missionary Alliance in 1887.

p. 187-188

a.   Simpson became a strong advocate of divine healing.

b.   Simpson was also a woman's advocate and facilitated the ministry of Spirit-led women.

    c.   Simpson expressed astounding insights related to the woman question.

Concerning the nature of God, he rejected the idea that God is male. He said that God is neither male nor female, but that God exhibits characteristics that we understand as masculine and feminine.

In one of his books, Simpson discusses "The Motherhood of God." He writes, "The heart of Christ is not only the heart of man, but has in it all the tenderness and gentleness of women."

He speaks metaphorically of the Holy Spirit as "our heavenly Mother," noting that the "Comforter assumes our nurture, training, teaching, and the whole direction of our life."

4.   Carrie Judd Montgomery (1848-1946), a colleague of Simpson, had been active in the healing movement since her healing in 1879 through Elizabeth Mix's ministry.

p. 188

    a.   She was the first woman to itinerate across America.

    b.   In 1890, Judd married George Montgomery, and in Oakland, California, opened the Home of Peace, the first West Coast healing home.

5.   Maria Woodworth-Etter (1844-1924) began evangelistic meetings in 1882.

p. 189
Show book.

a.   During her 40-year ministry, she preached to crowds of 25,000.

b.   These meetings were characterized by signs and wonders.

E.   Summary   p. 189

In the Healing Revival of the later nineteenth century, women were in leadership along with, in cooperation with, and independent of men. From the independent faith healing homes to the great healing meetings, the women of God were visible. The Holy Spirit anointing on their lives was the one outstanding feature that made room for them.

V.   SUMMARY OF THE 19TH CENTURY

A.   The Holy Spirit, working through the interwoven movements of the 19th century, advanced the status of women.   p. 189

B.   The direction of the activity of the Spirit was always toward equality, elevation, and liberation of women.   p. 190

C.   This activity occurred both inside the institution and outside the parameters of the institution in the Church at large.   p. 190

D.   Seth Cook Rees, founder of the Pilgrim Holiness Church, represents a host of men and women, who, by the 1890s, were advocating either inclusion of or equality for women in the Church, the home, and society at large.   p. 190

Read his remark.

VI.   THE EARLY PENTECOSTAL REVIVAL.   Chapter 12 begins here.

A.   Overview

1.   During the first decade of the early Pentecostal Revival (especially 1901-07), a unique blend of theological forces converged producing a rare time of equality for women in ministry and marriage.

2.   More specifically, the elements for equality in the revival were embodied in the leaders of the revival: Charles Fox Parham (1873-1929) and Sarah Thistlethwaite Parham (1877-1937), and Lilian Thistlethwaite (1873-1939).

B.   The 20th C. Pentecostal Revival began in the 1900 New Years' Eve Watchnight at Bethel Bible College, in Topeka, Kansas.

p. 191-192

C.   For about the next five years, the pioneers of Pentecost were Parham disciples either directly or indirectly.

p. 191
p. 193-194

The Parhams, Charles and Sarah, together with Sarah's sister, Lilian, benefited from a unique blend of elements from the Holiness, Wesleyan-Methodist, Quaker, Missionary, and Healing Movements. These characteristics, I would suggest, qualified them to be pivotal figures in the Pentecostal Revival and as advocates of biblical equality.

To get an intimate, first-hand view of the early revival, read The Life of Charles Fox Parham by his wife, Sarah Parham. Much of current information is filled with misinformation.

Show book and photos.

D.   Aspects of Parhams' Theology.

1.   Two primary factors shaped the Parhams' theology: prayerful reading of the Bible and experiences with the Holy Spirit that empowered them to live an overcoming life of faith.

p. 194-199

2.   In addition, the strong Quaker influence and intentional interaction with theological trends of the day helped shape their views.

3.   They believed in an old-fashioned conversion experience and a subsequent sanctification experience.

4.   They taught divine healing as being in the atonement, not because they had read about it in religious books, but because they had experienced God's healing power through faith in the Gospel.

5.   Maintaining an end-time perspective, they anticipated global revival followed by the soon return of the Lord. In view of this, they believed that the purpose of a modern Pentecost was the same as that of the original Pentecost (Acts 2:4): empowerment for missions.

6.   Ecclesiastically, although the Parhams did not reject denominationalism, they did avoid institutionalism.

7.   Ministry was the expression of personal experience with God in the Word and in the Holy Spirit. "The power that was to accompany Pentecost was not foolish, ridiculous, insane, fleshly performances, but the power to witness."

8.   This is what contributed to the remarkable egalitarian atmosphere of the early Pentecostal Revival. The inclusivism of the Methodist approach was overridden by the Quaker beliefs of equality in both marriage and ministry. Gender was not the determining factor; the Holy Spirit and giftings were.

E.   Hosts of Women Were at the Forefront of the Pentecostal Revival.   pp. 199-206

Draw what is appropriate from pp. 199-206.

F.   Summary Remarks

1.   In the early Pentecostal Revival, the determining factors in ministerial function and in the specific nature of the marriage relationship were the unique personality of each man and woman and the manifest activity of the Holy Spirit in the life of the individual.

2.   Authority was not determined by gender, but by the God-ordained expression of the Holy Spirit through the individual person.

3.   Especially among Parham disciples, in great part due to the strong egalitarian Quaker beliefs, it was normal for men and women to relate as equals in both marriage and ministry.

4.   Today the Pentecostal/Charismatic Movement is no longer egalitarian in terms of church or marriage.

For the move away from this biblical equality, read Chapter 13, pp. 209-230.

This tremendous, twentieth century outpouring has periodically ebbed in strength, but it has continued in resurgent tidal waves even to the present time. Now numbering 540 million adherents, and growing at the phenomenal rate of 24 million per year, this 100-year-old movement is the second largest group in Christendom, being outnumbered only by the centuries-old Roman Catholic Church. Sadly, however, the truly egalitarian quality of the early Revival has been lost. Are we willing to recover it?

VII.   PRAYER OF CONSECRATION AND COMMITMENT TO WALK WITH GOD

APPLICATION AND ENRICHMENT PROJECTS

1.   If the Declaration of Sentiments was not available in class, procure your own personal copy from http://www.luminet.net/~tgort/convent.htm.

2.   Peruse the National Women's History Project online at http://www.nwhp.org. Notice what a tremendous work this group is doing, but also note that the Christian aspect of many of their heroines have been "written out."

3.   Secure your own Susan B. Anthony Silver Dollar as a reminder of what one woman of faith, trusting in God, can do.

4.   Read Ruth Tucker and Walter Liefeld's book, <u>Daughters of the Church: Women and Ministry from New Testament Times to the Present</u> (Grand Rapids: Zondervan, 1987). Especially note the chapter on women in missions.

5.   Read Sarah Parham's book <u>The Life of Charles Fox Parham</u> (Joplin: Tri-State Printing, 1930) to get a first-hand sense of the Pentecostal outpouring at the turn of the century. Be especially aware of the women mentioned.

6.   Continue to add to your photo gallery of women of faith. Seek photos in books and online. Digital photographs are available from the Library of Congress.

7.   This course is too brief to deal with everything, but on your own time, read Chapters 13 and 14 (pp. 209-230) in the textbook to gain insight into why biblical equality was replaced by hierarchy and patriarchy in the Pentecostal and Charismatic Movements.

8.   Write a one-page (250 word) essay on the material in this lesson, placing emphasis on the part(s) that were most interesting or useful to you. Your paper should be double-spaced and should be typed in 12-point, Times Roman font. This will constitute page 7 of a paper that may be considered part of your final grade in this course.

FOR STUDY AND REVIEW

PART I

Based on the teaching in this lesson, indicate if the following statements are true or false by inserting a T or an F in the space provided.

1. ____ Hosts of women were at the forefront of the Pentecostal Revival.

2. ____ The Holy Spirit had nothing to do with the move toward equality for women in the 19th century.

3. ____ Women's missionary societies emerged and flourished apart from the churches.

4. ____ Women were not prominent in the healing movement.

5. ____ The Spirit-led advance toward equality for women occurred both inside and outside the parameters of the local church institutions in the Church at large.

PART II

Complete the sentences by selecting the best answers from the following list:

> ** Lottie Moon ** Phoebe Palmer ** A. J. Gordon ** Susan B. Anthony **
> ** A. B. Simpson ** Elizabeth Cady Stanton ** Hannah Whitall Smith **
> ** Mary Slessor ** Ann Hasseltine Judson ** Amy Carmichael **

1. Quaker women, _____ and _____, were the leading players in the effort in America to gain women's right to vote.

2. _____, the Quaker who authored The Christian's Secret to a Happy Life, was convinced that suffrage was a Christian cause and also staunchly advocated biblical equality in marriage.

3. _____, _____, _____, and _____ were outstanding pioneers and heroes of faith in the Missionary Movement.

4. Dr. Charles Cullis, the single, most important figure in the Healing Movement, received his sanctification experience in 1862 through _____'s ministry.

5. _____, founder of Gordon College and a Boston pastor of great intellectual and spiritual stature, was an ardent supporter of important social action including women's equal rights, and his 1894 work, The Ministry of Women, remains and important statement of support for women.

6. Christian and Missionary Alliance founder, _____, expressed astounding insights regarding women's equal biblical status and wrote a book in which he discusses "the Motherhood of God."

INT'L CHRISTIAN WOMEN'S HISTORY PROJECT

Writing God's Women Back into History

What is ICWHP?

ICWHP is the Int'l Christian Women's History Project, a multi-faceted project that can best be described as a resource center serving as a focal point for the writing, publication, collection, preservation, and dissemination of material regarding Christian women's history and women in God's plan. It is a vehicle for the revival and reformation of the Church and society.

How are ICWHP's Purposes Acheived?

The purposes of ICWHP are achieved through the direction of the Holy Spirit and the cooperation of those who understand the need and share the vision.

ICWHP:

- Conducts a center highlighting Christian women, past and present known as the Int'l Christian Women's Hall of Fame.

- Maintains an ever-growing library related to Christian women.

- Organizes research material about Christian women and issues related to Christian womanhood.

- Conducts seminars, conferences, and classes and develop courses.

- Maintains a speaker/teacher bureau.

- Publishes high quality educational materials.

Why ICWHP?

ICWHP exists to:

- Promote the Gospel Message of Jesus which includes the equality of women in terms of substance and value, function and authority, privilege and responsibility.

- Recognize Christian women living and deceased who have made significant contributions in the Church and in society in general.

- Inform women, the Church, and the world about Christian women's history.

- Preserve information in order to pass it along to new believers and to future generations.

- Preserve this data in one accessible location.

- Provide access to accurate sources of Christian women in history.

- Inspire faith and hope in women in order to strengthen them to fulfill God's specific assignments in their lives.

Where is ICWHP?

The administrative offices, research center and publication department share office space with Hyatt Int'l Ministries in the Dallas-Fort Worth Metroplex.

CONTACT: Dr. Susan Hyatt
P. O. Box 764463
Dallas, TX 75376
E-Mail: ICWHP@aol.com

How Can You Participate?

Here are just a few suggestions:

☑ Take initiative by indicating your interest and ask questions and contribute ideas.

☑ Nominate women for the **Int'l Christian Women's Hall of Fame** and for the *Int'l Biographical Dictionary of Christian Women's History*. Send for Nomination Forms nd make sure your favorite women (alive or deceased) are included.

☑ Contribute financial support toward the realization of ICWHP's purposes.

☑ Contribute books, photos, and other material that can be shared by others through the central resource center.

☑ Make yourself available to speak to groups interested in knowing more about God's women.

☑ Form a local study group to pray for God's women and to learn more about God's plan for His women.

☑ Share the news of ICWHP with others.

☑ Offer to research and write grant proposals.

☑ Volunteer to file material.

☑ Promote The Spirit, The Bible, & Women Conferences.

☑ Pray for God's plan for ICWHP to be fulfilled!

The Int'l Biographical Dictionary of Christian Women's History

One of ICWHP's first projects is *The Int'l Biographical Dictionary of Christian Women's History* (ISBN 1-888435-10-0). The concept of this book is being refined, but ICWHP anticipates a very interesting, informative, and readable book of high quality. A format of 1000 pages is the goal and the proposed publication date depending on participation and available resources.

YOU can become a contributing writer. Simply nominate women you know personally or through your study of history. Send for NOMINATION GUIDELINES to assist in this process. If you feel inadequate fulfilling the requirements alone, form a team of people to accomplish the task. But don't let one woman you deem worthy be left out!

Please, don't wait to be invited to participate! It is a team effort by men and women from around the world. I anticipate serving as your partner as a research guide, editor, and publisher, but I see a host of men and women participating to make this project a reality—a reality that will bless the Church.

An infinite number of small, inspirational biographies are also planned. Perhaps you would like to write one!

> The Spirit of the Lord is upon Me
> Because He has anointed Me
> to preach the gospel to the poor.
> He has sent Me to heal the brokenhearted,
> To preach deliverance to the captives
> And recovery of sight to the blind,
> To set at liberty
> those who are oppressed,
> To preach the acceptable year
> of the Lord
> (Lk. 4:18-19).

LESSON 8

What Does Genesis Really Say about Women?

LESSON 8

What Does Genesis Really Say about Women?

❑ THEME: Genesis teaches the full equality of women with men.

❑ PURPOSE: To gain a more accurate interpretation of passages in Genesis that have to do with beliefs about biblical womanhood.

❑ OBJECTIVES:

    1.   To understand that God is a Spirit, not a man or male form.

    2.   To correct the translation of Gen. 2:18, 20.

    3.   To correct the translation of Gen. 3:16.

    4.   To liberate men and women from false interpretations related to men and women in Genesis.

    5.   To follow the example of Jesus in terms of hermeneutics by going to God's original plan as revealed in Gen. 1 and 2 as opposed to Moses (esp. Deut. 24) when Jesus said, "But from the beginning it was not so" (Mt. 19:8).

❑ TEXTBOOK READING: Chapter 15, pp. 233-244.

❑ SUGGESTED READING AND TEACHING RESOURCES:

    •   Bushnell, Katherine. God's Word to Women. Mossville, IL: God's Word to Women Publishers, Reprint. N.d.

    •   Gundry, Patricia. "Why We're Here." Ed. Alvera Mickelsen. Women, Authority, and the Bible. Downers Grove: IVPress, 1986.

    •   Hull, Gretchen Gaebelein. "The Image of God: Women and Men as Social Equals." The ABC's of Gender Equality. Minneapolis: CBE, 1990. Pp. 4-6.

    •   Hyatt, Eddie L. "Back to the Beginning," p. 123 of this manual.

    •   Phillips, J. B. Your God Is too Small. New York: MacMillan, 1972. Pp. 21-22, 23-26, 53-55.

❑ LECTURE OUTLINE:

I.   PRINCIPLES

A.   Principle: What Genesis Says Will Be in Harmony with the Inner Witness and Historical Activity of the Holy Spirit.

B.   Principle: How We Understand the Bible Often Has to Do with What We Have Been Taught.

C.   Principle: It Is Not Easy to See Something from a New Perspective Even When that Different Perspective Is Correct. (Insert Woman Illusion Exercise)

D.   Principle: Jesus said the Holy Spirit Would Lead Us into All Truth (Jn. 16:13).

E.   Principle: Jesus Said to Go Back to the Beginning to Gain Insight and Correct Understanding (Mt. 19:8).

II.   MADE IN GOD'S IMAGE
      (Gen. 1:26-29; 2:18-24)

A.   Genesis 1:26-29.

1.   God made humanity as man and woman in His image.

2.   We must not make God in our image.

3.   Since God is Spirit, He does not have gender, thus the image of God has nothing to do with masculine or feminine (Jn. 4:23-24).

4.   God gave them both—male and female—responsibility and authority over creation, but not over one another (Gen. 1:26-28).

The Word and the Spirit agree. The activity of the Spirit constantly moving women in the direction of equality confirms the egaliatarian interpretation of Scripture. This interpretation is confirmed consistently by the best research into the text and culture of the era in which the text was written.

Review the woman-illusion diagram Lesson 1, p. 9.

Refer to the article by Eddie L. Hyatt on p. 131 at the end of this lesson.

p. 233

p. 233
God as a "projected image" of man or woman is a false image of God. See J. B. Philips, Your God Is too Small (pp. 53-54)

B.   Genesis 2:18-25.

    1.   Principle 1: The man and woman
        are made of the same substance.   p. 234

        This biblical truth stands in
        opposition to the pagan idea that
        woman is made of a substance
        inferior to that of the man.

    2.   Principle 2: The man and the   p. 234
        woman constitute a social unit.

        Verse 24 says that because of this
        male/female unit that God has
        ordained, a man is to leave his
        parents and together with a woman,
        establish a new social unit. Neither
        is to identify any longer with the
        their parental social units. They are
        to identify with one another.

    3.   These principles have implications: p. 234

        a.   This oneness reiterates the
            mandate expressed in
            Genesis 1:28 that they are
            both to have dominion over
            creation.

        b.   It reinforces the notion that
            this dominion is not over one
            another.

        c.   It is to be expressed equally
            through both individually
            since there is no indication of
            a breakdown of this mandate
            into a higher male authority
            and a lesser female authority.

III.   WOMAN: ADAM'S RIB AND HELPER   p. 235
    (Gen. 2:18, 20)

A.   The Rib Myth

    1.   The Hebrew word translated "rib"

occurs 42 times in the OT, and the only time it is translated "rib" is in this one reference to Eve

    2.   In every case but Gen. 2:21 in reference to Eve, it is translated "side" or "sides."

                    p. 235

    3.   Another Hebrew word is, in fact, the legitimate word for "rib" (Dan. 7:5).

                    p. 235

    4.   The "rib" translation of the Hebrew word meaning "side(s)" is rooted in the tradition of the rabbis. (235-36)

B.   Eve as "Side"

                    p. 236

    1.   The correct translation, "side(s)," indicates that woman came from the same substance and "source" (kephale) as man.

    2.   God took a side of Adam and created Eve.

    3.   The result was "flesh of his flesh and bone of his bone."

C.   Eve as "Helper"

    1.   The English word "helper" in this passage is the Hebrew word derived from the root 'ezer (aw-zar') meaning "to surround, protect, aid, help, succor."

    2.   This would indicate, then, that woman is man's protector who surrounds him and nurtures him. This is the opposite of "helper" or "helpmeet" meaning "servant" or "servanthood."

    3.   'ezer (ay'-zer) is used 14 times in the OT to refer to God.

    4.   It is also used twice to refer to Eve.

D.   Eve as "Suitable Helper"   p. 237

    1.   Genesis 2:18, in the Hebrew, reads
        <u>'ezer kenegdo.</u>

    2.   This expression means "one who is
        the same as the other and who
        surrounds, protects, aids, helps, and
        supports."

    3.   Compare this with the King James
        Version which translates it as "a
        helper meet for him."

    4.   Think about this! How different it is
        from the traditional, patriarchal or
        complementarian version!

    5.   There is clear indication of
        interdependence in this passage, but
        there is no suggestion of hierarchical
        separation of male and female
        spheres of responsibility, authority,
        or social roles.

IV.   HE SHALL RULE?   p. 237-238
    (Gen. 3:16)

A.   Genesis Does Not Teach that God Cursed
      Woman with Subordination.

    1.   This notion arose during the period   Familiarize yourself with
        between the end of the OT and the   the story of Pandora.
        beginning NT when the Jews, in an
        effort to reconcile the teaching of
        their Scriptures with Greek
        paganism, mingled the biblical story
        of Eve with the classical myth about
        Pandora.

    2.   The first reference to Eve as evil   p. 238
        (like Pandora) and as the source of
        evil occurs in the Apocryphal book,
        <u>Ecclesiasticus 25:24</u>, in about 250
        B.C.

3.   This has led to the normally unquestioned, traditional translation of Genesis 2:16 as:

> To the woman He [God] said: "I will greatly multiply your sorrow and your conception; in pain you shall bring forth children; Your desire shall be for your husband, And he shall rule over you."

B.   Gen. 3:16a

1.   The traditional translation is: p. 238-239

> I will greatly multiply your sorrow and your conception; in pain you shall bring forth children.

2.   The correct rendering of the sentence is: p. 239

> A snare hath increased thy sorrow and sighing.

3.   Satan had laid a snare that would result in much sorrow for the woman, and since the Messiah would be born of woman, Satan would henceforth challenge every birth, and so, "in pain she would bring forth children."   p. 239

C.   Gen. 3:16b

1.   The traditional translation is: p. 240

> Your desire shall be for your husband and he shall rule over you.

2.   As Dr. Bushnell correctly explains, this translation "has been made the keystone of an arch of doctrine subordinating woman to man, without which keystone the arch itself falls to pieces" (par. 139).   p. 240

3.   The search for truth must begin with the Hebrew word <u>teshuqa</u>. This is the word traditionally translated "desire"   p. 240-241

and sometimes "lust" or "lustful appetite."

4. The true meaning of this Hebrew word, however, is "turning" with no implication whatsoever of "desire" or "lust."   p. 240

5. Therefore, what this portion of the passage is saying is this: Eve is turning away from God toward her husband, and God is warning her that this turning will result in her coming under the domination of her husband (par. 136).

6. All of the best ancient versions of the Old Testament, including the Septuagint, render teshuqa with the idea of "turning."

7. A distortion of the meaning of this passage arose through the influence of the Talmud which is a compilation of the traditions of the Jews.

8. The teaching that God cursed Eve, and through her, all women, comes, not from the original Hebrew version of Genesis 3:16, but from the Babylonian Talmud, which, in fact, teaches ten curses of womanhood.   p. 241

9. The fifth curse is, "Thy desire shall be unto thy husband."   p. 241

10. The teaching of the seventh and eighth curses has also been allowed to cast a shadow forward into the NT so as to pervert the meaning of Paul's words about "covering" in 1 Cor. 11.

11. The distortion was first introduced by Jerome through his Latin translation of the Bible known as the Latin Vulgate (A.D. 382).   p. 241-242

D.   A valid rendering of Genesis 3:16 is: p. 242

A snare has increased your sorrow and sighing. In sorrow you shall bear sons/children. You will turn toward your husband and he will rule over you.

1.   God spoke no curse on Eve.   p. 242-243

2.   This is not a rule God is laying down, but a prediction of what would happen whenever Eve would put a man between herself and God; that is, she would be subject to this cursed fruit of disobedience. It was not a statement of God's original intent, desire, will, or plan, but a warning of the fruit of human-centered behavior.

3.   If, in fact, God did curse both man and woman, Christian men and women must remember that Jesus Christ has delivered both from any such penalty and redeemed both from any such judgment.

V.   CONCLUSION   p. 243

A.   In Creation, God Did Not Set Up a Male-Dominated Hierarchy.

B.   In the Fall, God Did Not Punish Eve with a Sentence of Subservience and Subjugation to Adam.

C.   These Ideas Crept through a Process of Mingling with Pagan Cultures and Subsequently Corrupted the Original Intent of Scripture.

APPLICATION AND ENRICHMENT PROJECTS

1.   Remember the biblical challenge to renew our minds (Rm. 12:2) and look again at the woman-illusion drawing in Lesson 2, page 9. Are you being transformed by the renewing of your mind in the biblically-based, historically-informed truth? If not, what is the hindrance? If so, in what ways are you aware of this renewing process?

2.   Obtain your personal copy of Katherine Bushnell's God's Word to Women. It is available from the web site http://wwwgodswordtowomen.org. It is set up in 100 Bible study lessons. Instead of merely reading it, do it as lessons over a period of time.

3.   Read and respond to the following report of a 1999 international, Pentecostal/Charismatic leaders conference as reported by Susan Hyatt.

        "In a recent international gathering of Pentecostal/Charismatic leaders, one bishop reminded the delegates that Adam's "listening to his wife" is the root of sin, and that men today must be careful not to be led by the "crackle" of a woman's voice. He shared how, when he was a child, his grandfather would warn him repeatedly that "Eve" is short for "Evil." His colleagues affirmed him and then warned the men that women are seductive and will readily accommodate the fall of ministers. On the feminine side of things, leading Charismatic women spent considerable time bolstering the male egos and conducted a women's luncheon that reinforced the secondary, subordinate, and inferior status of woman."

4.   Respond to the following remarks by J. B. Phillips in Your God Is too Small:

        "But surely, it may be objected, Christ Himself taught us to regard God as a Father. Are we to reject His own analogy? Of course not, so long as we remember that it is an analogy. When Christ taught His disciples to regard God as their Father in Heaven He did not mean that their idea of God must necessarily be based upon their ideas of their own fathers. For all we know there may have been many of His hearers whose fathers were unjust, tyrannical, stupid, conceited, feckless, or indulgent. It is the relationship that Christ is stressing. The intimate love for, and interest in, his son possessed by a good earthly father represents to men a relationship that they can understand, even if they themselves are fatherless! The same sort of relationship, Christ is saying, can be reliably reckoned upon by man in his dealings with God. . . . There are Christians who do not appear to understand this properly. . . We must leave behind the 'parental hangover' if we are to find a 'big enough' God" (pp. 22-23).

5.   Write a one-page (250-word) essay on the material in this lesson, placing emphasis on the part(s) that were most interesting or useful to you. Your paper should be double-spaced and should be typed in 12-point, Times Roman font. This will constitute page 8 of a paper that may be considered part of your final grade in this course.

FOR STUDY AND REVIEW

PART I

Based on the teaching in this lesson, indicate if the following statements are true or false by inserting a T or an F in the space provided.

1.   ___ How we understand the Bible often has to do with what we have been taught.

2.   ___ Genesis teaches that only the male is made in the image of God.

3.   ___ The idea of the subjugation and subservience of womanhood crept in through a mingling with pagan cultures.

4.   ___ A valid rendering of Gen. 3:16 is: "A snare has increased your sorrow and sighing. In sorrow you shall bear sons/children. You will turn toward your husband and he will rule over you."

5.   ___ In Creation, God set up a male-dominated hierarchy/chain-of-command social order.

PART II

Complete the sentences by selecting the best answers from the following list:

** teshuqa ** Jesus ** Genesis ** ezer ** God **

1.   What _____ really says will be in harmony with the inner witness and the historical activity of the Holy Spirit.

2.   _____ said that the Holy Spirit would lead us into all trugh (Jn. 16:13).

3.   The English word helper in Gen. 2:18, 20 is the Hebrew word derived from the root _____ meaning "to surround, protect, aid, help, succor" and it is used 14 times to refer to God and twice to refer to Eve.

4.   The idea that _____ cursed woman with subordination arose during the period between the OT and the NT when the Jews, in an effort to reconcile the teachings of their Scriptures with Greek paganism, mingled the biblical story of Eve with the classical myth about Pandora.

5.   The word _____ in Gen. 3:16b, which has been traditionally translated "lust" or "desire" really means simply "turning." Thus the accurate meaning of this passage is that Eve is turning away from God to her husband, and God is warning her that this turning will result in her coming under the domination of her husband.

BACK TO THE BEGINNING

By Eddie L. Hyatt, D.MIN., M.DIV., M.A.

Matt. 19:1-9 records a discussion between Jesus and the Pharisees concerning divorce. This discussion was prompted by the question posed by the Pharisees:
"Is it lawful for a man to divorce his wife for just any reason?"

This question was based on Deut. 24:1 which stated that if a man had become displeased with his wife because he had found some uncleanness in her, then he could write her a certificate of divorce and send her away. Because this passage left a lot of latitude for personal interpretation, Jewish men of Jesus' day had been known to divorce their wives over some very trivial matters. Perhaps because Jesus was showing an "unheard of" openness to women, the Pharisees posed this question as a challenge to Him. Jesus' answer reveals a very intriguing approach to Biblical interpretation that has far-reaching ramifications for a theology of womanhood.

Jesus replied,

"Have you not read that He who made them at the beginning made them male and female and said, 'For this reason a man shall leave his father and mother and be joined to his wife and the two shall become on flesh?' So then, they are no longer two but one flesh. Therefore, what God has joined together, let not man separate."

There Pharisees then quoted Deut. 24:1 and challenged, Why then did Moses command to give a certificate of divorce and send her away. Jesus replied, "Moses because of the hardness of your hearts permitted you to divorce your wives, but from the beginning it was not so."

Jesus answer reveals that He considered the Divine model for male-female relationships to be in Genesis account of creation, not in later passages that deal with relationships in a fallen world and culture. Moses, He said, permitted you to divorce your wives "because of the hardness of your hearts." The point is that we should not settle for that which God has tolerated or allowed because of our sin and hard hearts. We should, rather, be seeking God's highest and best for male-female relationships which is revealed in the creation accounts before sin entered the world. In other words, let's go back to the original model and not settle for later models that were offered to accommodate the sinfulness and fallenness of men and women. Let's go back to the beginning.

LESSON 9

What Does Paul Really Say about Women?

LESSON 9

What Did Paul Really Say About Women?

❑ THEME: The writings of Paul teach equality, not hierarchy.

❑ PURPOSE: To gain accurate interpretations of the NT passages typically used to subordinate women thus finding harmony with Genesis and Jesus.

❑ OBJECTIVES:

    1.   To demonstrate that the writings of Paul are in harmony with the rest of the Bible regarding the issue of equality.

    2.   To examine the biblical meaning of authority and of the terms headship, submission, covering.

    3.   To discover the egalitarian translations of passages used to subordinate women.

❑ TEXTBOOK READING: Chapter 16, pages 245-266

❑ SUGGESTED READING AND TEACHER RESOURCES:

- Bilezikian, Gilbert. "Subordination in the Godhead: A Re-emerging Heresy." Audiocassette, CBE. Wheaton: July 29-Aug. 1, 1993.

- Fee, Gordon. Commentary on the First Epistle to the Corinthians. Grand Rapids: Eerdmans, 1987.

- Kroeger, Richard Clark and Catherine Clark Kroeger. I Suffer Not a Woman: Rethinking 1 Timothy 2:11-15 in Light of Ancient Evidence. Grand Rapids: Baker, 1992.

- Kroeger, Catherine Clark. "Wifely Submission in Biblical Context." Included on pages 149-150 of this manaul.

- Mickelsen, Berkeley and Alvera. "Does Male Dominance Tarnish Our Translations?" Christianity Today. Oct. 5, 1979: 26.

- ___. "The 'Head' of the Epistles." Christianity Today. Feb. 20, 1981: 20-23.

- Scholer, David M. "Issues in Biblical Interpretation." The Evangelical Quarterly 88: 1 (1988): 21-22.

- Wilshire, Leland Edward. "The TLG Computer and Further Reference to authentein in 1 Timothy 2:12." New Testament Studies 34 (1988): 120-34.

❑ LECTURE OUTLINE:	QUESTIONS, NOTES, AND TEXTBOOK REFERENCES

I.   INTRODUCTION   p. 245

     A.   Genesis Shows that God Intended an Egalitarian Model for Human Relationships.   From Ch. 15 in text and Lesson 8 in manual

          1.   This model was disrupted in the fall by the probability that the woman would tend to turn her attention away from God to man.

          2.   Hierarchy, therefore, became the norm for fallen humanity.

          3.   Although matriarchy is sometimes the expression of this hierarchy, patriarchy is the usual expression since men have tended to prevail.

     B.   When Jesus Came, He Taught an Egalitarian Model.   From Ch. 2 and Lesson 2

     C.   At Pentecost, the Holy Spirit fell equally on men and women, thereby reinforcing the egalitarian model of Genesis and Jesus.   From Ch. 3 and Lesson 2

          1.   The Spirit did not communicate with woman through man.

          2.   The Spirit related equally and directly to both.

     D.   We Can, Therefore, Confidently Expect that the Model to Be Found in the Epistles Will also Be Egalitarian.

          1.   Lesson 2 explored the egalitarian model of the New Testament.

          2.   This lesson explores the words and passage of the Epistles traditionally used to enforce hierarchy, and especially, patriarchy.

II.   HEADSHIP IN THE EPISTLES
        (1 Cor. 11:2-16; Eph. 5:21-33)

        A.   The Greek Word, <u>Kephale</u>, ("Head")
                Indicates No Chain-of-Command Meaning
                or Hierarchical Intent.

                1.   <u>Kephale</u> ("Head") does not mean   p. 245
                        "head" in the sense of "authority
                        over" or "leadership," (1 Cor. 11:2-
                        16; Eph. 4:15, 23; 5:21-33; Col.
                        1:18; 2:10, 18).

                2.   Extensive research clearly indicates   p. 247
                        that <u>kephale</u> means "source of life"
                        (in creation), a meaning entirely void
                        of the idea of authority.

                3.   <u>Kephale</u> clearly refers to the fact that
                        woman came out of Adam in
                        creation. Paul says that man was the
                        source of woman in Creation and
                        now woman is the source of man in
                        procreation, and Christ is the Source
                        of Life for both men and women
                        (1 Cor. 11).

                4.   Liddell, Scott, Jones, and McKenzie (<u>A</u>   p. 247
                        <u>Greek-English Lexicon</u>, 9th ed.,
                        Clarendon Press, 1940) renders the
                        meaning of <u>kephale</u> as "source" with
                        no implication of hierarchy or
                        authority.

                5.   In the <u>Septuagint</u>, whenever the idea   p. 247-249
                        of authority over or rulership is
                        intended, the word used is <u>archon</u>,
                        not <u>kephale</u>

                6.   David M. Scholer, who has produced   p. 249
                        the definitive essay on <u>kephale</u>,
                        concludes that <u>kephale</u> "does not
                        support the traditionalist or
                        complementarian view of male
                        headship and female submission."
                        He states, "This data supports a new
                        understanding in Christ by which

men and women are viewed in a mutually supportive, submissive relationship."

7.   Catherine Kroeger observes that the egalitarian renderings of <u>kephale</u> agree with the overall tone of equality and mutuality expressed in over fifty New Testament passages.

                                                  p. 249-250

B.   Marriage in the Greco-Roman World.   p. 250

1.   In the Greco-Roman world, homosexuality was considered superior to heterosexual relationships because women were "unclean, evil, inferior, and unequal."

2.   When Paul wrote 1 Cor.11:11-12, he was communicating with people incultured with these beliefs, and he what he was actually doing was affirming heterosexual marriage.

    a.   By declaring man to be the <u>kephale</u> ("source") of woman—not the <u>archon</u> ("ruler")—Paul was denouncing the pagan notion that woman was of a lesser substance than man.

    b.   By declaring man to be the <u>kephale</u> ("source") of woman—not the <u>archon</u> ("ruler")—Paul was saying that woman was indeed a fit partner for man.

    c.   Paul thus confirms this equality and then speaks of a mutuality between man and woman when he continues, "Neither is the woman independent of the man nor the man of the woman in the Lord; for just as the woman is from man, so man is from the woman, and all things are of God" (1 Cor. 11:11-12).

3. Paul's references to marriage in Ephesians 5 must also be placed in historical, cultural perspective.

p. 251

    a. The common marriage form in the Roman Empire was <u>sine manu</u> marriage.

    b. A woman in this pagan style of marriage remained officially attached to her birth patriarch, and was not an official member of her husband's household.

    c. Paul writes Eph. 5 to instruct new believers that Christian marriage is the formation of a new and distinct social unit.

    d. This passage has to do with God's intention of intimacy and oneness between husband and wife, and in no way promotes authoritative male rulership and female subordination.

D. Colossians 1:18-23 and 2:10, 19.

p. 253

1. In 1:18, <u>kephale</u> refers to Christ being the First and, therefore, the Source of the Church. "He is the Source of the body of believers, the Church."

2. In 2:10, we are told we are "complete in Him, who is the Source of all principality and power."

3. In 2:19, we are warned not to be diverted by those things that would break our connection with

Our Source or that would, in any way, hinder the flow of Life.

4.   In Colossians, therefore, as in Ephesians, kephale means "source" and carries no sense of authority over or rulership.

E.   1 Corinthians 11:3   p. 253-254

But I want you to know that the kephale of every man is Christ; the kephale of woman, man; and the kephale of Christ, God.

1.   Paul's intended meaning revolves around the meaning of kephale.

2.   If we substitute the accurate meaning of kephale in this verse, it would read as follows: "But I want you to know that the source of every man is Christ; the source of woman, man; and the source of Christ, God."

3.   This translation was also proposed by, among other early theologians, Cyril of Alexandria (A.D. 376?-444).

4.   Another consideration in understanding Paul's intention in this verse is the non-hierarchical structure of his statement.

5.   If it were a statement intended to indicate a chain-of-command, it should read: "God is the archon of Christ is the archon of man is the archon of woman.

6.   Another problem regarding the hierarchical interpretation is that it requires a hierarchy in the Godhead.

F.   Conclusion.   p. 255

1.   Paul used kephale in Ephesians and Colossians to mean "source," not authority over."

2. <u>Kephale</u> does not mean "authority over" in 1 Corinthians.

3. To impose meanings other than Paul's, from outside the context in which he wrote, is to read into his writings something that he did not intend and that the Scripture, accurately interpreted, does not mean.

III. **SUBMISSION**
(Eph. 5:18-22)

p. 255-256

Entwined with the doctrine of authoritative male headship is the teaching on female submission.

A. The Meaning of Hupotasso.

"Submit" is the English used to translate the Greek word <u>hupotasso</u> in the NT.

1. <u>Hupotasso</u> can mean "to show responsible behavior toward others."

p. 256

2. <u>Hupotasso</u> can mean "to be brought into a sphere of influence."

p. 256

3. <u>Hupotasso</u> can mean "to add or unite one person or thing with another."

p. 245

B. Paul's Use of the Household Code.

p. 257

1. Paul found it necessary to advise his converts about family relationships (Eph. 5), beginning with something they understood (Household Code) and leading them to something different from what they had known, that is, <u>Christian</u> marriage.

2. In Eph. 5:18-33, Paul is describing Christian marriage, asking husband and wife to be committed to one another only (v. 31) in an atmosphere of mutual identification and unity (v. 21).

a.   He asks a married woman to
identify with (<u>hupotasso</u>) and
be committed to her husband
rather than to her birth
family.

b.   He asks children and slaves
to obey (<u>hupakouo</u>).

c.   He asks a husband to love
(<u>agape</u>) his wife (a new idea)
and to submit (<u>hupotasso</u>) to
his wife (v. 21).

3.   Unilateral obedience and subjugation   p. 257
of the wife to the husband is not a
biblical doctrine.

4.   The issues here are identity and unity   p. 257-258
(husband and wife as a cohesive unit
of equal partners), sameness of
substance, and equality in value.

5.   Accurately interpreted, the passage   p. 258
does not promote authoritative male
dominance and female subjugation.

C.   Considerations in Eph. 5:15-18.   p. 258-259

1.   Beginning in Eph. 4, Paul is
instructing the believers how to live,
and in 5:15-18, he is telling them that
this means they are to walk in
wisdom and to be filled with the
Spirit.

2.   The principal verb in the passage is   p. 258
<u>be filled</u> (v. 18); that is, "Be filled
with the Spirit . . .."

3.   This main verb is followed by five   p. 258
present participles that describe how
a person would behave when filled
with the Spirit: addressing (v. 19a),
singing (v. 19b), making (v. 19b),
giving (v. 20), and being subject to
one another . . .." (v. 21).

4.   Be filled with the Spirit (v. 18) . . .
     submitting to one another (v. 21) . . .
     wives to your own husbands (v.22).

     a.   This clearly speaks of   p. 258-259
          mutuality, not hierarchy.

     b.   V. 22, referring to the wife's
          relation with her husband,
          reads, "wives to your own
          husbands."

     c.   Because v. 22 does not
          contain a verb, it cannot be a
          unilaterial command and
          cannot stand on its own
          because the overriding
          context is "submitting to one
          another" (v. 21).

IV.   COVERING
(1 Cor. 11:3-16)

A.   Covering Is a Covenant Word.   p. 259

Under the Old Covenant, the blood of goats
and lambs was the covering for sin. It only
covered the sin; it did not erase it. Under
the New Covenant, the Blood of Jesus is our
covering. It doesn't just cover over sin; it
erases sin and eradicates the sin nature!

B.   Various Groups Interpret Covering   p. 259
     According to Their Unique Perceptions

     1.   Mennonites insist that it means that
          women must always wear a
          headcovering, a bonnet, a specific
          style of cap.

     2.   Holiness people insist that it means
          that women must not cut their hair.

     3.   In the Discipleship Movement
          (1970s), the idea of "covering" as
          "authority over" came into the
          Charismatic Revival in relation to
          personal, domestic, and discipleship
          situations.

4.   In the 1990s, the same doctrine of "covering" as "authority over" thrives under the idea of unilateral accountability, an idea that is nowhere taught in NT Christianity.

B.   The Central Verse is 1 Corinthians 11:10:   p. 260

Therefore the woman ought to have authority over her own head because of the angels [or messengers].

1.   Both the NKJV and the NIV read "a sign of authority" where the Greek should be translated "to have authority."

2.   The insertion of the words "a sign" is a grave error.

3.   The Living Bible rendering: "So a woman should wear a covering on her head as a sign that she is under man's authority," is totally in error.

4.   Gordon Fee concludes that Paul "is   p. 260-261 affirming the 'freedom' of women over their own heads."

V.   THE ISSUE OF AUTHORITY   p. 261
       (1 Tim. 2:12)

I do not permit women to teach or to have authority over a man; she must be silent" (Tim. 2:12).

A.   The Apparent Prohibition of a Woman   p. 261 Teaching a Man

1.   In the broader context of the New Testament it is clear that women did teach both men and women.

2.   This, then, is addressing a unique situation in Ephesus.

B.   The Apparent Prohibition of a Woman   p. 261-162 Having Authority over a Man

1. This has been used by some to teach that women can prophecy but cannot judge prophecy because in doing so the woman might be exercising authority over a man.

2. Jesus clearly stated that we are not to exercise authority over one another (Mt. 20:25-26).

3. In Genesis, God did not give man authority over woman, nor woman over man, but He gave them both authority over creation.

C. The Meaning of the Word Authentein

1. The English word "authority" in this verse is the Greek word authentein.

2. This is the only occurrence of the word authentein in the NT.

3. This word always carried connotations of violence and the meaning of "murder" or "murderer."

4. 1 Timothy 2 is confronting a problem in Ephesus wherein a fusion of Gnosticism and worship of the goddess, Artemis, was promoting the idea that, in Creation, Eve had been the source (kephale) of Adam.

VI. "LORD" ABRAHAM
(1 PETER 3:6)

A. Sarah Called Abraham "Lord."

Sarah obeyed Abraham and called him "lord" (1 Pet. 3:6), a reference to Gen. 20:1-18.

1. The Greek word that is translated "obeyed" is derived directly from the verb "to listen," and for that reason, may just as accurately be translated "listened attentively to."

Mt. 8:5-13 is often used to justify hierarchy, but a careful reading of the story shows that the issue is the power of the spoken word over sickness, not the control of one person over another person. This agrees with Gen. 1:26-28. Also to teach this (Mt. 8:5-13) as chain-of-command in human relationships is to have Jesus contradict Himself by teaching the ways of the Gentiles in this case after firmly stating (Mt. 20:25-26) that we are not to follow the ways of the Gentiles.

Authentein explanation is on pp. 262-263.

For explanation of 4., refer to p. 263

p. 263

2.   Sarah called Abraham <u>kurion</u> meaning "lord, master, or sir," a word that was commonly used to show common courtesy, not authority over.

B.   God Called Sarah Abraham's <u>Ba'al.</u>

"But God came to Abimelech in a dream by night, and said to him, 'Behold, thou art but a dead man for the woman which thou hast taken; for she is a man's wife.'"

1.   This is the only place in the OT that the word <u>ba'al</u> is translated "wife" instead of "lord, master, owner. "

2.   God called Sarah, Abraham's "lord, master, owner."

C.   The Context Speaks of Mutuality in both OT and NT Passages.

1.   The idea of mutuality is apparent when God commanded Abraham to heed his wife's advice (Gen. 21:12).

2.   The structural context of 1 Peter 2 and 3 suggests mutuality.

The idea of respect is the real theme and it begins in verse 11 and particularly in verse 13, "Submit yourselves. . . ." A pattern is apparent in 3:1, <u>likewise</u>, wives . . . ; and 3:7, <u>likewise</u>, husbands. . . . This appears to be encouraging the same mutuality, identification with, and unity observed in Eph. 5:18-22.

VII.   CONCLUSION

A.   The Biblical Evidence Supports Mutual Submission, not Unilateral Hierarchy.

B.   Refer to David M. Scholer's Statement.

---

p. 264

Some discussion surrounds Gen. 20:3. The verb form (as a participle) and the noun form appear in verse 3, and it may, in fact, be a construct that could be rendered, "the woman who is married to a husband." For this, see <u>Brown, Driver, Briggs, and Gesenius</u> <u>Hebrew and English Lexicon</u> (Peabody: Hendrickson, 1979), 127a and 127b. However, Millard Erickson writes, "To be sure, the Hebrew world בַּעַל (ba'al), meaning 'lord' or 'master,' is frequently used for husband. It should also be observed, however, that the feminine form that word also appears. In Genesis 20:3, for example, it is used to describe Sarah's relationship to Abraham." Millard J. Erickson, <u>Christian Theology</u> (Grand Rapids: Baker, 1985), 547. The actual meaning remains unclear.

p. 265

Read quote on p. 265.

APPLICATION AND ENRICHMENT PROJECTS

1.   Read Chapter 17, <u>How Does Culture Condition?</u>, on pp. 267-272 in the textbook.

2.   Review George Fox's understanding of <u>headship</u>. For a thorough understanding, read his essays in his <u>Journal</u>. Some of these are listed in the textbook, pp. 103-113. Notice that without the help of modern Conservative scholarship, he was able to harmonize the meaning of headship as non-authoritarian, rulership, or responsibility over, with the egalitarian principles of Jesus and the Holy Spirit.

3.   Read Catherine Kroeger's article, "Wifely Submission in Biblical Context." (Copy included on the following page by permission of the author.)

4.   Read the article by Alvera and Berkeley Mickelsen entitled "The 'Head' of the Epistles." <u>Christianity Today</u>. Feb. 20, 1981: 20-23. This would be available in any good, theological library or by request from <u>Christianity Today</u>.

5.   Continue to build your personal library by including books such as:

    •   Fee, Gordon. <u>Commentary on the First Epistle to the Corinthians.</u> Grand Rapids: Eerdmans, 1987.

    •   Kroeger, Richard Clark and Catherine Clark Kroeger. <u>I Suffer Not a Woman: Rethinking 1 Timothy 2:11-15 in Light of Ancient Evidence</u>. Grand Rapids: Baker, 1992.

6.   Subscribe to <u>The Priscilla Papers</u> edited by Gretchen Gaebelin Hull and published by Christians for Biblical Equality, 122 W. Franklin Ave., Ste. 218, Minneapolis, MN 55404. <u>http://www.cbeinternational.org</u> or 1(877) 285-2256.

7.   Write a one-page (250-word) essay on the material in this lesson, placing emphasis on the part(s) that were most interesting or useful to you. Your paper should be double-spaced and should be typed in 12-point, Times Roman font. This will constitute page 8 of a paper that may serve as part of your final grade in this course.

FOR STUDY AND REVIEW

PART I

Based on the teaching in this lesson, indicate if the following statements are true or false by inserting a T or an F in the space provided.

1. ____ Since Genesis, Jesus, and Acts teach equality, Paul brings balance by teaching hierarchy, or the secondary status of the woman to the man in terms of authority in marriage and ministry.

2. ____ The Greek word <u>kephale</u> ("head") indicates a chain-of-command meaning.

3. ____ In 1 Cor. 11, Paul says that man was the source of woman in Creation and now woman is the sources of man in procreation, and Christ is the Source of Life for both men and women.

4. ____ By declaring man to be the <u>kephale</u> ("source") of woman—not the <u>archon</u> ("ruler")—Paul was saying that woman was denouncing the pagan notion that woman was made of a lesser substance than man.

5. ____ The idea of "submission" in marriage is always presented in the sense of mutuality, not in the sense of authority.

PART II

Complete the sentences by selecting the best answers from the following list:

**   hupotasso   ** kephale   ** hupakouo   * archon   **
**   mutual submission   ** egalitarian   ** authentein   **

1. _____ does not mean "head" in the sense of authority over or leadership, whereas the word _____ does carry this meaning, so if Paul had been talking about a man having authority over a woman, or one person having authority over another person, he would have chosen _____ rather than _____.

2. Paul asks a married woman to identify with _____, not come under the authority of her husband as opposed to identifying with her birth family, and he asks children and slaves to obey _____.

3. Ephesians 5:15-18, accurately read, teaches mutual submission, that is, "submitting to one another," not the benevolent rulership of the man over the woman. This _____ way of life is based on "Be filled with the Spirit" (v. 18).

4. _____ is a covenant word based on the idea of the Blood Covenant taking away sin; therefore, the idea in the New Covenant refers to the Blood of Jesus forgiving and erasing sin from the life of the believer. It has nothing to do with "authority over" or "accountability to."

5. In 1 Tim. 2:12, Paul used the word _____, the only time this word is used in the New Testament, to refute ideas of female superiority coming from the cult of Artemis (Diana) in Ephesus.

WIFELY SUBMISSION IN BIBLICAL CONTEXT

By Catherine Clark Kroeger, PH.D.

All too often people fail to grasp the balanced biblical teaching on the subject because they fail to study the material in its immediate context; nor do they try to understand how the material relates to the totality of Scripture. Few areas have suffered more from these omissions than the subject of wifely submission.

There is indeed a dictate in the Bible "that every man should be ruler over his own household." But this decree (Esther 1:22) was formulated by the tyrannical pagan King Ahasuerus and his injudicious advisors. Ahasuerus is later villainously persuaded to add a second decree, that all Jews in his empire should be exterminated. The book of Esther is the story of how a courageous and faith-filled woman negotiates a reversal of those decrees. She risks her life to enter into the king's presence uninvited, an act of civil and marital disobedience. With the prayerful support of her people, she uses her wits, skill and charm to win deliverance for the Jews. Then Esther "wrote with full authority" (Est. 9:29) to establish the celebration of Purim. "Esther's decree confirmed these regulations about Purim, and it was written down in the records" [of the Persian Empire] (Est. 9:32). Both of the king's decrees have been overthrown, and Esther stands as a woman and a Jew who has gained the respect and support of her husband.

She is the only woman in the Bible to follow the leading of God rather than that of her husband. Abigail, a wise and beautiful woman, realizes that the behavior of her churlish spouse has endangered the lives of all the males in their household. In defiance of her husband's insulting action toward David, she rushes to undo the damage. As she is bearing gifts to effect a reconciliation, she meets David at the head of a war party, intent upon annihilating her family. Her wisdom and good sense cause David to exclaim, "Praise be to the Lord, the God of Israel, who has sent you today to meet me. May you be blessed for your good judgement and for keeping me from bloodshed" (1 Sam. 25:32-33). Though Abigail's stupid husband dies in a fit of rage, the rest of the family has been saved by her intervention. In deed, the early church considered her a prophet because of her understanding and proclamation of God's purpose for David (see 1 Sam. 25:28-31).

Other godly women made decisions that were honored by their husbands as well as their communities and were blessed by God (1 Sam. 1:21-24;

2 Kings 4:8-13; Prov. 31:16-20). Sarah, by compliance with her husband Abraham's unwise instructions, brought misfortune on others and reproach upon the people of God (Gen. 12:10-20; 20:2-18), whereas Abraham was specifically instructed by God to follow the dictate of his wife (Gen. 21:12). In the early church, Priscilla and Aquila appear to have functioned in their marriage and ministry as fully equal partners, in contrast to foolish Sapphira who suffered the consequences of following her husband's deceitful stratagem (Acts 5:1-10).

The Bible represents women as responsible individuals, capable of making good decisions and of thereby growing into maturity. In an analogy to marriage, Christ is depicted as a bridegroom implementing the full development of the bride's potential, including the full development of the bride's potential, including the ability to make her own decisions (Eph. 5:25-27). Jesus specifically deplored one person's claiming ascendancy over another (Mt. 20:25-28; Mk. 10:42-45) and declared that it hindered intimacy (Jn. 15:15). The concepts "headship" and "submission" are translations of Greek terms that had quite different connotations in their original contexts; great care should be taken in applying them to modern marriage. Notably, each New Testament mandate for a woman's submission is *always* within a context of equality and mutual submissions (1 Cor. 7:3-5; Eph. 5:18-33; Col. 3:13-19; 1 pet. 2:16-3:8) along with a strong injunction against marital abuse (Eph. 5:28-29; Col. 3:19; 1 pet. 3:7).

Far from placing the woman in a restrictive position, Scripture empowers and affirms women both as individuals and within marital relationships. Christianity is based upon mutuality, interdependence, and equality of all members (Eph. 5:21; Gal. 5:13; 1 pet. 5:5). Equally shared decision-making is the pattern sanctified by Scripture and proven effective in human experience.

(Catherine Clark Kroeger is Christians for Biblical Equality President Emerita and adjunct professor at Gordon Conwell Theological Seminary. She is author, along with her husband Richard Kroeger, of I Suffer Not a Woman.)

Used by permission of the author.

LESSON 10

How Should We Then Live?

LESSON 10
How Should We Then Live?

❏ THEME: The Spirit and the Word present the equality of women with men in substance, value, authority, and function, and recognition of this fact will affect the way we think (theologize) about and behave in relation to women.

❏ PURPOSE: To summarize and bring practical application while bringing closure to the study.

❏ OBJECTIVES:

1.   To summarize the fact that the Bible and the Holy Spirit teach the equality of men and women in substance and value, function and authority, privilege and responsibility.

2.   To explore reasons why people reject biblical equality.

3.   To offer practical guidelines for egalitarian living.

4.   To evaluate effectiveness of this course.

❏ TEXTBOOK READING: Chapter 19, pp. 291-300, and Chapter 20, 301-304.

❏ SUGGESTED READING AND TEACHER RESOURCES:

CBE Statement: Men, Women & Biblical Equality.
    http://www.cbeinternational.org or CBE, 122 W. Franklin Ave., Ste. 218, Minneapolis, MN 55404-2451. http://www.cbeinternational.org or 1 (877) 285-2256.

Hubbard, M. G. and J. Hubbard, Ph.D. "Psychological Resistance to Egalitarianism." Journal of Biblical Equality 2, (1990): 26-52. Contact CBE for copies of this or for information about how to contact Drs. Hubbard for copies.

❑ LECTURE OUTLINE:

QUESTIONS, NOTES, AND
TEXTBOOK REFERENCES

I.   REVIEW

    A.   Genesis Teaches Equality.

        1.   Genesis shows that God created woman as equal in substance and value, function and authority, privilege and responsibility.

        2.   Genesis shows that God intended equality in man-woman relationships.

            This model was disrupted in the fall by the probability that the woman would tend to turn her attention away from God to man. Hierarchy, therefore, was the predictable norm for fallen humanity.

    B.   Jesus Reinforced and Affirmed the Equality of Women in What He Said and Did.

    C.   The Holy Spirit Continued Jesus' Message of Equality.

        1.   On the Day of Pentecost, the Holy Spirit fell equally on men and women for the same purpose.

        2.   The Holy Spirit did not and does not communicate with woman through man, but He relates equally and directly to both.

        3.   The writings of Paul, correctly interpreted, teach equality of men and women in substance and value, function and authority, privilege and responsibility.

    D.   History Reveals that the Church Adopted a Theology of Womanhood Heavily Influenced by Pagan Principles of Woman as Inferior, Evil, Unequal, and Unclean.

E.   The Activity of the Spirit in History Affirms the Equality of Women in Substance and Value, Function and Authority, Privilege and Responsibility.

II.   DEALING WITH RESISTANCE   p. 291

A.   Roots of Resistance

Although biblical womanhood is usually debated in theological terms, the argument frequently has little to do with the Bible or theology because it is about power and control.

Note remarks by Walter Liefeld and Timothy Weber in textbook.

1.   Prejudice.   p. 292

Resistance to female equality in some men appears to be related to the internalized stereotype that has become part of self-identity.

Refer to the notes in the textbook taken from Drs. Gay and Joseph Hubbards' article,. "Psychological Resistance to Egalitarianism."

2.   Power.

Resistance to female equality is also bound up in a man's perception of power and the threat of losing that power.

3.   Pride.   p. 293

Resistance to female equality is also bound up in "the strong sense of entitlement which the hierarchical position grants to males, and which in Highly Resistant Males produces a distorted sense of pride."

4.   Privilege.   p. 293

Resistance to female equality is bound up in the Highly Resistant Male's idea of being privileged, a sense derived from, among other things, an incorrect understanding of biblical headship.

III.   BIBLICAL PRINCIPLES AND PRACTICES

    A.   Principles of Biblical Relationships   p. 296-297

        1.   Regard

        2.   Respect

        3.   Respond

    B.   Practices of Biblical Equality   The CBE statement is
                                                          included, by permission
       Refer to CBE.'s Men, Women and Biblical   from Christians for Biblical
       Equality, Application on pp. 157-158.   Equality.

IV.   EXIT QUESTIONNAIRE   Included on the pp. 159-
                                                          160 and in tear-out form in
    The Exit Questionnaire should be administered at   Appendix B to be
    this point. Turn in the copy in Appendix B.   submitted to the teacher.

V.   CLOSING REMARKS

    A.   Biblical Equality Is about Biblical
        Responsibility, Not Privilege.

    B.   The Subjugation of Women is Not Biblical,   A reading of Chapter 20,
        Logical or Acceptable.   pp. 301-304 would be
                                                            effective, together with any
    C.   The Church—More than Any Other Group   comments by the teacher.
        in the World—Should Be Promoting Gender
        Equality Because It Is Part of Jesus' Gospel   This could be followed by
        Message.   a time of testimony, prayer,
                                                          and rejoicing.
    D.   Let the Church Be the Church of the Lord
        Jesus Christ!

       Only when the Church renounces captivity
       and discrimination within, can it minister
       true freedom to the captives without. Only
       when it sets free its own slaves will the world
       take seriously its preaching of liberty. Only
       then will it begin to realize the full power
       inherent in the gospel.

MEN, WOMEN AND BIBLICAL EQUALITY

Statement by Christians for Biblical Equality (Used by Permission)

The Bible teaches the full equality of men and women in Creation and in Redemption (Gen. 1:26-28, 2:23, 5:1-2; 1 Cor. 11:11-12; Gal. 3:13, 28, 5:1).

The Bible teaches that God has revealed Himself in the totality of Scripture, the authoritative Word of God (Matt. 5:18; John 10:35; 2 Tim. 3:16; 2 Peter 1:20-21). We believe that Scripture is to be interpreted holistically and thematically. We also recognize the necessity of making a distinction between inspiration and interpretation: inspiration relates to the divine impulse and control whereby the whole canonical Scripture is the Word of God; interpretation relates to the human activity whereby we seek to apprehend revealed truth in harmony with the totality of Scripture and under the guidance of the Holy Spirit. To be truly biblical, Christians must continually examine their faith and practice under the searchlight of Scripture.

BIBLICAL TRUTHS

Creation

1) The Bible teaches that both man and woman were created in God's image, had a direct relationship with God, and shared jointly the responsibilities of bearing and rearing children and having dominion over the created order (Gen. 1:26-28).

2) The Bible teaches that woman and man were created for full and equal partnership. The word "helper" (ezer) used to designate woman in Genesis 2:18 refers to God in most instances of Old Testament usage (e.g. 1 Sam. 7:12; Ps. 121:1-2). Consequently the word conveys no implication whatsoever of female subordination or inferiority.

3) The Bible teaches that the forming of woman from man demonstrates the fundamental unity and equality of human beings (Gen. 2:21-23). In Genesis 2:18, 20 the word "suitable" (kenegdo) denotes equality and adequacy.

4) The Bible teaches that man and woman were co-participants in the Fall: Adam was no less culpable than Eve (Gen. 3:6; Rom. 5:12-21; 1 Cor. 15:21-22).

5) The Bible teaches that the rulership of Adam over Eve resulted from the Fall and was therefore not a part of the original created order. Genesis 3:16 is a prediction of the effects of the Fall rather than a prescription of God's ideal order.

Redemption

6) The Bible teaches that Jesus Christ came to redeem women as well as men. Through faith in Christ we all become children of God, one in Christ, and heirs to the blessings of salvation without reference to racial, social, or gender distinctives (John 1:12-13; Rom. 8:14-17; 2 Cor. 5:17; Gal. 3:26-28).

Community

7) The Bible teaches that at Pentecost the Holy Spirit came on men and women alike. Without distinction, the Holy Spirit indwells women and men, and sovereignly distributes gifts without preference as to gender (Acts 2:1-21; 1 Cor. 12:7, 11, 14:31).

8) The Bible teaches that both women and men are called to develop their spiritual gifts and to use them as stewards of the grace of God (1 Peter 4:10-11). Both men and women are divinely gifted and empowereed to minister to the whole Body of Christ, under His authority (Acts 1:14; 18:26; Rom. 16:1-7, 12-13, 15; Phil. 4:2-3; Col. 4:15; see also Mark 15:40-41, 16:1-7; Luke 8:1-3; John 20:17-18; compare also Old Testament examples: Judges 4:4-14, 5:7; 2 Chron. 34:22-28; Prov. 31:30-31; Micah 6:4).

9) The Bible teaches that, in the New Testament economy, women as well as men exercise the prophetic, priestly and royal functions (Acts 2:17-18, 21:9; 1 Cor. 11:5; 1 Peter 2:9-10; Rev. 1:6; 5:10). Therefore, the few isolated texts that appear to restrict the full redemptive freedom of women must not be interpreted simplistically and in contradiction to the rest of Scripture, but their interpretation must take into account their relation to the broader teaching of Scripture and their total context (1 Cor. 11:2-16, 14:33-36; 1 Tim. 2:9-15).

10) The Bible defines the function of leadership as the empowerment of others for service rather than as the exercise of power over them (Matt. 20:25-28, 223:8; Mark 10:42-45; John 13:13-17; Gal. 5:13; 1 Peter 5:2-3).

Family

11) The Bible teaches that husbands and wives are heirs together of the grace of life and that they are bound together in a relationship of mutual submission and responsibility (1 Cor. 7:3-5; Eph. 5:21; 1 Peter 3:1-7; Gen. 21:12). The husband's function as "head" (kephale) is to be understood as self-giving love and service within this relationship of mutual submission (Eph. 5:21-23; Col. 3:19; 1 Peter 3:7).

12) The Bible teaches that both mothers and fathers are to exercise leadership in the nurture, training, discipline and teaching of their children (Exod. 20:12; Lev. 19:3; Deut. 6:6-9; 21:18-21, 27:16; Prov. 1:8, 6:20; Eph. 6:1-4; Col. 3:20; 2 Tim. 1:5; see also Luke 2:51).

APPLICATION

Community

1) In the church, the spiritual gifts of women and men are to be recognized, developed and used in serving and teaching ministries at all levels of involvement: as small group leaders, counselors, facilitators, administrators, ushers, communion servers, and board members, and in pastoral care, teaching, preaching, and worship. In so doing, the church will honor God as the source of spiritual gifts. The church will also fulfill God's mandate of stewardship without the appalling loss to God's kingdom that results when half of the church's members are excluded from positions of responsibility.

2) In the church, public recognition is to be given to both women and men who exercise ministries of service and leadership. In so doing, the church will model the unity and harmony that should characterize the community of believers. In a world fractured by discrimination and segregation, the church will dissociate itself from worldly or pagan devices designed to make women feel inferior for being female. It will help prevent their departure from the church or their rejection of the Christian faith.

Family

3) In the Christian home, husband and wife are to defer to each other in seeking to fulfill each other's preferences, desires and aspirations. Neither spouse is to seek to dominate the other but each is to act as servant of the other, in humility considering the other as better than oneself. In case of decisional deadlock they should seek resolution through biblical methods of conflict resolution rather than by one spouse imposing a decision upon the other. In so doing, husband and wife will help the Christian home stand against improper use of power and authority by spouses and will protect the home from wife and child abuse that sometimes tragically follows a hierarchical interpretation of the husband's "headship."

4) In the Christian home, spouses are to learn to share the responsibilities of leadership on the basis of gifts, expertise, and availability, with due regard for the partner most affected by the decision under construction. In so doing, spouses will learn to respect their competencies and their complementarity. This will prevent one spouse from becoming the perennial loser, often forced to practice ingratiating or deceitful manipulation to protect self-esteem. By establishing their marriage on a partnership basis, the couple will protect it from joining the tide of dead or broken marriages resulting from marital inequities.

5) In the Christian home, couples who share a lifestyle characterized by the freedom they find in Christ will do so without experiencing feelings of guilt or resorting to hypocrisy. They are freed to emerge from an unbiblical "traditionalism" and can rejoice in their mutual accountability in Christ. In so doing, they will openly express their obedience to Scripture, will model an example for other couples in quest of freedom in Christ, and will stand against patterns of domination and inequality sometimes imposed upon church and family.

We believe that biblical equality as reflected in this document is true to Scripture.

We stand united in our conviction that the Bible, in its totality, is the liberating Word that provides the most effective way for women and men to exercise the gifts distributed by the Holy Spirit and thus to serve God.

Gilbert Bilezikian, W. Ward Gasque, Stanley N. Gundry, Gretchen Gaebelein Hull, Catherine Clark Kroeger, Jo Anne Lyon, Roger Nicole.

CHRISTIAN FOR BIBLICAL EQUALITY
122 West Franklin Avenue, Suite 218,
Mpls, MN 55404-2451
Phone (612) 872-6898 Fax (612) 872-6891
E-Mail: cbe@cbeinternational.org
www.cbeinternational.org

V.   EXIT QUESTIONNAIRE

<u>Instructions</u>:   Circle the response that most closely describes your belief. A space following each statement provides room for the student to make a brief comment if this would be helpful.

1. YES. NO. I DON'T KNOW. I believe God has male gender.

2. YES. NO. I DON'T KNOW. I believe husbands are to exercise authority over their wives.

3. YES. NO. I DON'T KNOW. I believe men are to exercise authority over women in ministry.

4. YES. NO. I DON'T KNOW. I believe woman as "helper" (or "help meet" or "help mate") in Genesis means that God calls women to be subordinate helpers of men.

5. YES. NO. I DON'T KNOW. I believe the word "submit" in Paul's writings means that women are to come under the authority of men.

6. YES. NO. I DON'T KNOW. I believe the Bible prescribes different roles for men and women based solely on gender.

7. YES. NO. I DON'T KNOW. I believe women are equal in substance but subordinate in function and authority.

8. YES. NO. I DON'T KNOW. I believe Jesus taught chain-of-command principles in relationships.

9. YES. NO. I DON'T KNOW. I believe women can prophesy but should not judge prophecy.

10. YES. NO. I DON'T KNOW. I believe Paul taught chain-of-command principles in relationships.

11. YES. NO. I DON'T KNOW. I believe there is subordination (chain-of-command) in the Trinity.

12. YES. NO. I DON'T KNOW. I believe qualified women should be able to occupy the top positions of authority in the Church.

13. YES. NO. I DON'T KNOW. I believe women should be able to teach men as well as women.

14. YES. NO. I DON'T KNOW. I believe women need an accountability "covering."

15. YES. NO. I DON'T KNOW. I believe women can be apostles.

16. YES. NO. I DON'T KNOW. I believe women can be prophets.

17. YES. NO. I DON'T KNOW. I believe women can be evangelists.

18. YES. NO. I DON'T KNOW. I believe women can be senior pastors.

19. YES. NO. Do you have unanswered questions about biblical womanhood? If so, list them.

20. YES. NO. I DON'T KNOW. Will this teaching make a difference in your life? Explain.

APPLICATION AND ENRICHMENT PROJECTS

1.   Read Chapter 18, pp. 275-289, to get an understanding of the feminist mission field that has been almost totally ignored by the Church. Once you have integrated the biblical truth regarding biblical womanhood, you can become a Spirit-led, sensitive, knowledgeable evangelist to this vast segment of the harvest.

2.   Find ways in your life to reinforce the truths you have learned in this course.

3.   Be sensitive to the leading of the Holy Spirit in communicating the truth of biblical equality to men and women in the Church.

4.   Continue to develop your bibliography and add to your library and files.

5.   Assimilate this material and teach it!

6.   Write a one-page (250-word) essay on the material in this lesson, placing emphasis on the part(s) that were most interesting or useful to you. Your paper should be double-spaced and should be typed in 12-point, Times Roman font. This will constitute page 10 of a paper that may be considered part of your final grade in this course.

FOR STUDY AND REVIEW

PART I

Based on the teaching in this lesson, indicate if the following statements are true or false by inserting a T or an F in the space provided.

1.   ___ Genesis shows that God created woman as equal in substance and value, function and authority, privilege and responsibility.

2.   ___ Jesus reinforced this equality of women in what He said and did.

3.   ___ The subjugation of women is biblical, logical, and mandated.

4.   ___ History reveals that the Church adopted a theology of womanhood heavily influenced by pagan principles of woman as inferior, evil, unequal, and unclean.

5.   ___ The activity of the Spirit in history affirms the equality of Women in substance and value, function and authority, privilege and responsibility.

PART II

Complete the sentences by selecting the best answers from the following list:

** privilege ** substance ** respect ** value ** power ** regard **
** pride function ** prejudice ** responsibility ** turn away **
** response ** egalitarian ** authority **

1.   Resistance to female equality in some people appears to be related to established ideas of _____, _____, _____, and _____.

2.   Three words that can help describe biblical relationships are _____, _____, and _____.

3.   Biblical equality is about _____, not _____.

4.   The _____ model of Genesis was disrupted in the fall by the probability that the woman would tend to _____ her attention from God to man; thus making hierarchy the predictable norm for fallen humanity.

5.   The Bible teaches that God's will for man and woman is equality in terms of _____ and _____, _____ and _____, _____ and _____.

APPENDIX 1

Entrance Questionnaire

ENTRANCE QUESTIONNAIRE

Name: _____ Did you attend all 10 lessons? _____

INSTRUCTIONS: Circle the response that most closely describes your belief.

1. I believe God is male gender.   Yes. _____   No. _____   I don't know. _____

2. I believe husbands are to exercise authority over their wives. YES. _____   NO. _____   I DON'T KNOW._____

3. I believe men are to exercise authority over women in ministry. YES. _____   NO. _____   I DON'T KNOW.

4. I believe that woman as "helper" (or "help meet" or "help mate") in Genesis means that God calls women to be subordinate helpers of men. YES. _____   NO. _____   I DON'T KNOW. _____

5. I believe the word "submit" in Paul's writings means women are to come under the authority of men. YES. _____   NO. _____   I DON'T KNOW. _____

6. I believe the Bible prescribes different roles for men and women based solely on gender. YES. _____   NO. _____   I DON'T KNOW. _____

7. I believe women are equal in substance but subordinate in function and authority. YES. _____   NO. _____   I DON'T KNOW. _____

8. I believe Jesus taught chain-of-command principles in relationships. YES. ____   NO. ____   I DON'T KNOW. ____

9. I believe women can prophecy but should not judge prophecy. YES. _____   NO. ____   I DON'T KNOW.____

10. I believe Paul taught chain-of-command principles in relationships. YES. _____   NO. _____   I DON'T KNOW.____

11. I believe there is subordination (chain-of-command) in the Trinity. YES. _____   NO. _____   I DON'T KNOW.____

12. I believe qualified women should be able to occupy the top positions of authority in the Church. YES. _____   NO. _____   I DON'T KNOW. _____

13. I believe women should be able to teach men as well as women. YES. ____   NO. ____   I DON'T KNOW._____

14. I believe women need an accountability "covering." YES. _____   NO. _____   I DON'T KNOW._____

15. I believe women can be apostles. YES. _____   NO. _____   I DON'T KNOW._____

16. I believe women can be prophets. YES. _____   NO. _____   I DON'T KNOW. ____

17. I believe women can be evangelists. YES. _____   NO. _____   I DON'T KNOW. _____

18. I believe women can be senior pastors. YES. _____   NO. _____   I DON'T KNOW. ____

19. I have studied Church history. YES. _____   NO. _____ If so, in your opinion, how much?

20. I have studied women in Church history. YES. _____   NO. _____ If so, in your opinion, how much?

APPENDIX 2

Exit Questionnaire

EXIT QUESTIONNAIRE

Name: _____ Did you attend all 10 lessons? _____

INSTRUCTIONS: Circle the response that most closely describes your belief.

1.   I believe God is male gender.
         YES. _____   NO. _____   I DON'T KNOW.   _____
         Comment, if necessary.

2.   I believe husbands are to exercise authority over their wives.
         YES. _____   NO. _____   I DON'T KNOW.   _____
         Comment, if necessary.

3.   I believe men are to exercise authority over women in ministry.
         YES. _____   NO. _____   I DON'T KNOW.   _____
         Comment, if necessary.

4.   I believe that woman as "helper" (or "help meet" or "help mate") in Genesis means that God calls
         women to be subordinate helpers of men.
         YES. _____   NO. _____   I DON'T KNOW.   _____
         Comment, if necessary.

5.   I believe the word "submit" in Paul's writings means women are to come under the authority of men.
         YES. _____   NO. _____   I DON'T KNOW.   _____
         Comment, if necessary.

6.   I believe the Bible prescribes different roles for men and women based solely on gender.
         YES. _____   NO. _____   I DON'T KNOW.   _____
         Comment, if necessary.

7.   I believe women are equal in substance but subordinate in function and authority.
         YES. _____   NO. _____   I DON'T KNOW.   _____
         Comment, if necessary.

8.   I believe Jesus taught chain-of-command principles in relationships.
         YES. _____   NO. _____   I DON'T KNOW.   _____
         Comment, if necessary.

9.   I believe women can prophecy but should not judge prophecy.
         YES. _____   NO. _____   I DON'T KNOW.   _____
         Comment, if necessary.

10.   I believe Paul taught chain-of-command principles in relationships.
       YES. _____   NO. _____   I DON'T KNOW.   _____
       Comment, if necessary.

11.   I believe there is subordination (chain-of-command) in the Trinity.
       YES. _____   NO. _____   I DON'T KNOW.   _____
       Comment, if necessary.

12.   I believe qualified women should be able to occupy the top positions of authority in the Church.
       YES. _____   NO. _____   I DON'T KNOW.   _____
       Comment, if necessary.

13.   I believe women should be able to teach men as well as women.
       YES. _____   NO. _____   I DON'T KNOW.   _____
       Comment, if necessary.

14.   I believe women need an accountability "covering."
       YES. _____   NO. _____   I DON'T KNOW.   _____
       Comment, if necessary.

15.   I believe women can be apostles.
       YES. _____   NO. _____   I DON'T KNOW.   _____
       Comment, if necessary.

16.   I believe women can be prophets.
       YES. _____   NO. _____   I DON'T KNOW.   _____
       Comment, if necessary.

17.   I believe women can be evangelists.
       YES. _____   NO. _____   I DON'T KNOW.   _____
       Comment, if necessary.

18.   I believe women can be senior pastors.
       YES. _____   NO. _____   I DON'T KNOW.   _____
       Comment, if necessary.

19.   Overall, has this course been helpful to you? Explain.

APPENDIX 3

Answer Key to
Lesson Study & Review Exercises

LESSON 1

PART I

Based on the teaching in this lesson, indicate if the following statements are true or false by inserting a T or an F in the space provided.

1.   _T_ Jesus is the only legitimate starting point for a biblically sound theology of womanhood.

2.   _F_ This course is only for women.

3.   _T_ Men can benefit from this course.

4.   _T_ Students of this course will probably encounter biblical truth about womanhood that will challenge ideas they have been taught by culture and religion.

5.   _T_ What we believe about womanhood determines what we believe women can and should experience in terms of relationships, opportunity, marriage, quality of life, self-esteem, and ministry.

PART II

Complete the sentences by selecting the best answers from the following list:

** Jesus ** biblical ** evil ** historical ** inferior ** message ** activity **
** renew ** unclean ** abusive ** repent ** unequal ** Spirit **

1.   This course draws on both **biblical** and **historical** studies.

2.   The Church's traditional way of thinking about womanhood was developed under the influence of the pagan concepts that woman is **evil**, **unclean**, **unequal**, and **inferior**.

3.   The Christian message regarding womanhood must reflect with integrity the **message** of **Jesus** as revealed in the Bible, accurately interpreted, and in Church history as revealed by the **activity** of the Holy **Spirit**, especially in times of revival.

4.   It can be shown that the traditional way of thinking about womanhood has produced **abusive** behavior toward women.

5.   Awakened to biblical truth about womanhood, perhaps for the first time, men and women will have the opportunity, if necessary, to **repent** and **renew** their minds.

LESSON 2

PART I

Based on the teaching in this lesson, indicate if the following statements are true or false by inserting a T or an F in the space provided.

1.   _T_ Jesus taught equality by what He said and what He did.

2.   _T_ The story of Ananias and Sapphira illustrates that God holds husbands and wives each individually, personally, and directly responsible to Him for their behavior.

3.   _T_ The believers in Acts demonstrate a remarkable tendency toward the equality Jesus taught.

4.   _F_ Women were not allowed to function as apostles.

5.   _T_ On occasion, Jesus projected God in the image of woman.

PART II

Complete the sentences by selecting the best answers from the following:

** Spirit ** marriage ** roles ** coworkers **
** ministry ** woman **

1.   Jesus demonstrated woman's equality in both **marriage** and **ministry**.

2.   Jesus rejected the notion that women are to be restricted to certain **roles**.

3.   The Risen Christ commissioned the first apostle—a **woman**.

4.   Euodia and Syntyche were **coworkers** with Paul who worked with him, not under him.

5.   The **Spirit** continued to advance the idea of equality of men and women in terms of substance and value, function and authority, privilege and responsibility.

LESSON 3

PART I

Based on the teaching in this lesson, indicate if the following statements are true or false by inserting a T or an F in the space provided.

1.   _T_ Throughout the centuries, the Holy Spirit has continued to renew true believers, and with these renewals have come efforts by the Spirit to democratize the Church and to reinstate the egalitarian status of women.

2.   _F_ To the extent that institutionalism replaced the leadership of the Holy Spirit, women were elevated to equality with men.

3.   _T_ In the New Testament, all believers are called both "clergy" (kleros) and "laity" (laos).

4.   _F_ The Church's rejection of revival through Montanism resulted in a corresponding elevation of women.

5.   _T_ The shift from Spirit-life and Biblical equality to institutionalism increased in the latter second century.

PART II

Complete the sentences by selecting the best answers from the following list:

** Maxmilla ** institutionalism ** Montanism ** Roman Empire **
** Montanists ** human control ** Tertullian ** Prisca **

1.   **Montanism** was the Church's first revival.

2.   In the early Church, **institutionalism** crept in at the expense of Spirit-life.

3.   The Church moved toward a patriarchal system of government derived, not from the teachings of Jesus, but identical in structure to the **Roman Empire**.

4.   Institutionalism is an emphasis on organization in which **human control** displaces the leadership of the Holy Spirit.

5.   **Tertullian** who, in his early writings spoke vehemently against women, joined the **Montanists** and modified his views, speaking respectfully of **Maxmilla, Prisca**, and a "gifted sister" in his congregation.

LESSON 4

PART I

Based on the teaching in this lesson, indicate if the following statements are true or false by inserting a T or an F in the space provided.

1.   _T_ The prevailing attitude of the Church fathers toward women was heavily influenced by the pagan idea that women are evil, unclean, inferior, and unequal.

2.   _T_ The Church of the Middle Ages taught that wife-beating was "chastisement" for disobedience and exhorted men to beat their wives and wives to kiss the rod that beat them..

3.   _F_ None of the women burned at the stake were Spirit-filled Christians.

4.   _T_ Protestantism's general rejection of the charismatic activity of the Spirit denied the elevating, equalizing effect of the Spirit.

5.   _F_ The Reformation revived the message of Jesus about womanhood.

6.   _F_ The Bible teaches that a man is the "high priest" and ruler of the home.

7.   _F_ Jesus taught that the basic unit of the Church is the home.

8.   _T_ The idea that the man is the ruler of the home was promoted by King James and the English Reformation as means of controlling society.

9.   _T_ "Priesthood of all believers" includes women.

10.   _T_ Political and personal agendas of Church leaders denied women equality.

PART II

Complete the sentences by selecting the best answers from the following list:

  ** witchcraft ** Socrates * Beguines ** Roman Ritual ** Aristotle ** Aquinas **

1.   Two Greek philosophers, **Socrates** and **Aristotle**, influenced the development of thinking about womanhood among early Church leaders.

2.   The **Beguines** were bold women of the Spirit during the Middle Ages.

3.   **Aquinas**, the official theologian of the Roman Catholic Church in the 13th century, believed that women "are defective and misbegotten" and totally inferior.

4.   In the **Roman Ritual** (A.D. 1000), the Roman Church had designated speaking in tongues as the chief evidence of demonic possession among the common folk.

5.   Some women who were accused of **witchcraft** were, in fact, Spirit-filled believers who refused to submit to the Church's effort to control the people.

LESSON 5

PART I

Based on the teaching in this lesson, indicate if the following statements are true or false by inserting a T or an F in the space provided.

1.   **T** Margaret Fell declared that opposition to women speaking comes from the spirit of darkness and apostasy that had been prevailing in the church for 1200 years.

2.   **T** Since God is no respecter of persons in that He has given each one the same potential to respond to Christ, the early Quakers believed that we are to treat all human beings with equal dignity and respect.

3.   **F** Susanna Wesley endorsed the mediatoral position of the Anglican church rathter than direct and personal obedience to the indwelling Holy Spirit.

4.   **T** William Penn said of George Fox: "He exercised no authority but over evil."

5.   **F** Only men were permitted to be leaders in Methodism.

PART II

Complete the sentences by selecting the best answers from the following list:

** Mary ** Susanna Wesley ** Friends ** Margaret Fell **
** George Fox ** John Wesley **

1.   The **Friends**, a Bible-believing, Spirit-filled revival people, were the first major advocates of biblical equality since the days of the New Testament.

2.   When George Fox met men who believed that women had no souls, "no more than a goose," he reminded them of the words of **Mary**: "My soul doth magnify the Lord" (Lk. 1:46).

3.   In 1666, **Margaret Fell** wrote Women Speaking Justified, the first major book written in favor of female public ministry.

4.   **George Fox** considered Christ the only "Head."

5.   Regarding women in ministry, **John Wesley** said, "Who am I that I should withstand God?"

6.   For various reasons, some consider **Susanna Wesley** to have been the true founder of Methodism.

LESSON 6

PART I

Based on the teaching in this lesson, indicate if the following statements are true or false by inserting a T or an F in the space provided.

1.   _T_ Nineteenth-century America saw a convergence of Spirit-motivated movements that elevated women toward equality.

2.   _F_ Catherine Booth said that the equality of women is "a remarkable device of the devil."

3.   _T_ The WCTU, a Christian women's movement for "the protection of the home," became the largest woman's organization in the world with works in 50 nations.

4.   _F_ Katherine Bushnell believed that educated women should remain silent and submitted to the "biased and erroneous biblical translations and commentaries."

5.   _T_ At least 3 Biblical themes promoting equality arose in the Holiness Movement: the Galatians 3:28 theme, the Redemption theme, and the Pentecostal theme.

PART II

Complete the sentences by selecting the best answers from the following list:

** Katherine Bushnell ** Catherine Booth ** Phoebe Palmer **
** Hannah Whitall Smith ** Frances Willard **

1.   Obedience to the call of God by **Phoebe Palmer** resulted in her becoming the most influential leader of the Holiness Movement.

2.   **Catherine Booth**, co-founder of the Salvation Army, was "an unfailing, unflinching, uncompromising champion of woman's rights" who staunchly refused to be considered or treated anything but equal with her husband.

3.   **Hannah Whitall Smith**, a Quaker who wrote the classic book The Christian's Secret of a Happy Life, was deeply involved in movements with special concerns for the welfare and equality of women in society and in marriage.

4.   The founder of the Woman's Christian Temperance Union, **Frances Willard**, drew her strength and direction from her personal relationship with the Lord.

5.   **Katherine Bushnell** wrote the classic book God's Word to Women.

LESSON 7

PART I

Based on the teaching in this lesson, indicate if the following statements are true or false by inserting a T or an F in the space provided.

1.   _T_ Hosts of women were at the forefront of the Pentecostal Revival.

2.   _F_ The Holy Spirit had nothing to do with the move toward equality for women in the 19th century.

3.   _T_ Women's missionary societies emerged and flourished apart from the churches.

4.   _F_ Women were not prominent in the healing movement.

5.   _T_ The Spirit-led advance toward equality for women occurred both inside and outside the parameters of the local church institutions in the Church at large.

PART II

Complete the sentences by selecting the best answers from the following list:

** Lottie Moon ** Phoebe Palmer ** Susan B. Anthony **
** A. B. Simpson ** Elizabeth Cady Stanton ** Hannah Whitall Smith **
** Mary Slessor ** A. J. Gordon ** Ann Hasseltine Judson ** Amy Carmichael **

1.   Quaker women, **Susan B. Anthony** and **Elizabeth Cady Stanton**, were the leading players in the effort in America to gain women's right to vote.

2.   **Hannah Whitall Smith**, the Quaker who authored The Christian's Secret to a Happy Life, was convinced that suffrage was a Christian cause and also staunchly advocated biblical equality in marriage.

3.   **Lottie Moon**, **Mary Slessor**, **Amy Carmichael**, and **Ann Hasseltine Judson** were outstanding pioneers and heroes of faith in the Missionary Movement.

4.   Dr. Charles Cullis, the single, most important figure in the Healing Movement, received his sanctification experience in 1862 through **Phoebe Palmer**'s ministry.

5.   **A. J. Gordon**, founder of Gordon College and a Boston pastor of great intellectual and spiritual stature, was an ardent supporter of important social action including women's equal rights, and his 1894 work, The Ministry of Women, remains and important statement of support for women.

6.   Christian and Missionary Alliance founder, **A. B. Simpson**, expressed astounding insights regarding women's equal biblical status and wrote a book in which he discusses "the Motherhood of God."

LESSON 8

PART I

Based on the teaching in this lesson, indicate if the following statements are true or false by inserting a T or an F in the space provided.

1.   **T** How we understand the Bible often has to do with what we have been taught.

2.   **F** Genesis teaches that only the male is made in the image of God.

3.   **T** The idea of the subjugation and subservience of womanhood crept in through a mingling with pagan cultures.

4.   **T** A valid rendering of Gen. 3:16 is: "A snare has increased your sorrow and sighing. In sorrow you shall bear sons/children. You will turn toward your husband and he will rule over you."

5.   **F** In Creation, God set up a male-dominated hierarchy/chain-of-command social order.

PART II

Complete the sentences by selecting the best answers from the following list:

** teshuqa ** Jesus ** Genesis ** ezer ** God **

1.   What **Genesis** really says will be in harmony with the inner witness and the historical activity of the Holy Spirit.

2.   **Jesus** said that the Holy Spirit would lead us into all truth (Jn. 16:13).

3.   The English word helper in Gen. 2:18, 20 is the Hebrew word derived from the root **ezer** meaning "to surround, protect, aid, help, succor" and it is used 14 times to refer to God and twice to refer to Eve.

4.   The idea that **God** cursed woman with subordination arose during the period between the OT and the NT when the Jews, in an effort to reconcile the teachings of their Scriptures with Greek paganism, mingled the biblical story of Eve with the classical myth about Pandora.

5.   The word **teshuqa** in Gen. 3:16b, which has been traditionally translated "lust" or "desire" really means simply "turning." Thus the accurate meaning of this passage is that Eve is turning away from God to her husband, and God is warning her that this turning will result in her coming under the domination of her husband.

LESSON 9

PART I

Based on the teaching in this lesson, indicate if the following statements are true or false by inserting a T or an F in the space provided.

1.   _F_ Since Genesis, Jesus, and Acts teach equality, Paul brings balance by teaching hierarchy, or the secondary status of the woman to the man in terms of authority in marriage and ministry.

2.   _F_ The Greek word kephale ("head") indicates a chain-of-command meaning.

3.   _T_ In 1 Cor. 11, Paul says that man was the source of woman in Creation and now woman is the sources of man in procreation, and Christ is the Source of Life for both men and women.

4.   _T_ By declaring man to be the kephale ("source") of woman—not the archon ("ruler")—Paul was denouncing the pagan notion that woman was made of a lesser substance than man.

5.   _T_ The idea of submission in marriage is always presented in the sense of mutuality, not in the sense of authority.

PART II

Complete the sentences by selecting the best answers from the following list:

** hupotasso ** kephale ** hupakouo ** archon **
** mutual submission ** egalitarian ** authentein ** covering **

1.   **kephale** does not mean "head" in the sense of authority over or leadership, whereas the word **archon** does carry this meaning, so if Paul had been talking about a man having authority over a woman, or one person having authority over another person, he would have chosen **archon** rather than **kephale**.

2.   Paul asks a married woman to identify with **hupotasso**, not come under the authority of her husband as opposed to identifying with her birth family, and he asks children and slaves to obey **hupakouo**

3.   Ephesians 5:15-18, accurately read, teaches mutual submission, that is, "submitting to one another," not the benevolent rulership of the man over the woman. This **egalitarian** way of life is based on "Be filled with the Spirit" (v. 18).

4.   **Covering** is a covenant word based on the idea of the Blood Covenant taking away sin; therefore, the idea in the New Covenant refers to the Blood of Jesus forgiving and erasing sin from the life of the believer. It has nothing to do with "authority over" or "accountability to."

5.   In 1 Tim. 2:12, Paul used the word **authentein** the only time this word is used in the New Testament, to refute ideas of female superiority coming from the cult of Artemis (Diana) in Ephesus.

LESSON 10

PART I

Based on the teaching in this lesson, indicate if the following statements are true or false by inserting a T or an F in the space provided.

1.   __T__ Genesis shows that God created woman as equal in substance and value, function and authority, privilege and responsibility.

2.   __T__ Jesus reinforced the equality of women in what He said and did.

3.   __F__ The subjugation of women is biblical, logical, and mandated.

4.   __T__ History reveals that the Church adopted a theology of womanhood heavily influenced by pagan principles of woman as inferior, evil, unequal, and unclean.

5.   __T__ The activity of the Spirit in history affirms the equality of women in substance and value, function and authority, privilege and responsibility.

PART II

Complete the sentences by selecting the best answers from the following list:

** privilege ** substance ** respect ** value ** power ** regard **
** pride function ** prejudice ** responsibility ** turn away **
** response ** egalitarian ** authority **

1.   Resistance to female equality in some people appears to be related to established ideas of **prejudice**, **power**, **pride**, and **privilege**.

2.   Three words that can help describe biblical relationships are **respect**, **regard** and **response**.

3.   Biblical equality is about **responsibility**, not **privilege**.

4.   The **egalitarian** model of Genesis was disrupted in the fall by the probability that the woman would tend to **turn away** her attention from God to man; thus making hierarchy the predictable norm for fallen humanity.

5.   The Bible teaches that God's will for man and woman is equality in terms of **substance** and **value**, **function** and **authority**, **privilege** and **responsibility**.

APPENDIX 4

Examination

FINAL EXAM – SHORT ANSWER

STUDENTS' NAME: _____ GRADE: ____/100

| PART I | (Value: 25 items @ 2 each = 50 points) |

Based on the teaching in this course, indicate if the following statements are true or false by inserting a T or an F in the space provided.

1. ___ Jesus is the only legitimate starting point for a biblically sound theology of womanhood.

2. ___ What we believe about womanhood determines what we believe women can and should experience in terms of relationships, opportunity, marriage, quality of life, self-esteem, and ministry.

3. ___ The story of Ananias and Sapphira illustrates that God holds husbands and wives each individually, personally, and directly responsible to Him for their behavior.

4. ___ The believers in Acts demonstrate a remarkable tendency toward the equality Jesus taught.

5. ___ Throughout the centuries, the Holy Spirit has continued to renew true believers, and with these renewals have come efforts by the Spirit to democratize the Church and to reinstate the egalitarian status of women.

6. ___ To the extent that institutionalism replaced the leadership of the Holy Spirit, women were elevated to equality with men.

7. ___ The prevailing attitude of the Church fathers toward women was heavily influenced by the pagan idea that women are evil, unclean, inferior, and unequal.

8. ___ The Bible teaches that a man is the "high priest" and ruler of the home.

9. ___ Margaret Fell declared that opposition to women speaking comes from the spirit of darkness and apostasy that had been prevailing in the church for 1200 years.

10. ___ Catherine Booth said that the equality of women is "a remarkable device of the devil."

11. ___ Katherine Bushnell believed that educated women should remain silent and submitted to the "biased and erroneous biblical translations and commentaries."

12.   ___ At least 3 Biblical themes promoting equality arose in the Holiness Movement: the Galatians 3:28 theme, the Redemption theme, and the Pentecostal theme.

13.   ___ Hosts of women were at the forefront of the Pentecostal Revival.

14.   ___ The Holy Spirit had nothing to do with the move toward equality for women in the 19th century.

15.   ___ How we understand the Bible often has to do with what we have been taught.

16.   ___ Genesis teaches that only the male is made in the image of God.

17.   ___ A valid rendering of Gen. 3:16 is: "A snare has increased your sorrow and sighing. In sorrow you shall bear sons/children. You will turn toward your husband and he will rule over you."

18.   ___ In Creation, God set up a male-dominated hierarchy/chain-of-command social order.

19.   ___ Since Genesis, Jesus, and Acts teach equality, Paul brings balance by teaching hierarchy, or the secondary status of the woman to the man in terms of authority in marriage and ministry.

20.   ___ The Greek word kephale ("head") indicates a chain-of-command meaning.

21.   ___ In 1 Cor. 11, Paul says that man was the source of woman in Creation and now woman is the sources of man in procreation, and Christ is the Source of Life for both men and women.

22.   ___ By declaring man to be the kephale ("source") of woman—not the archon ("ruler")—Paul was denouncing the pagan notion that woman was made of a lesser substance than man.

23.   ___ The idea of submission in marriage is always presented in the sense of mutuality, not in the sense of authority.

24.   ___ The subjugation of women is biblical, logical, and mandated.

25.   ___ The activity of the Spirit in history affirms the equality of women in substance and value, function and authority, privilege and responsibility.

PART II   (Value: 8 items @ 2 each = 16 points)

Complete the sentences by selecting the best answers from the following list:

** Jesus ** Spirit ** Montanists ** Aquinas **
** marriage ** coworkers ** ministry ** woman **

1.   The Christian message regarding womanhood must reflect with integrity the message of _____ as revealed in the Bible, accurately interpreted, and in Church history as revealed by the activity of the Holy Spirit, especially in times of revival.

2.   Jesus demonstrated woman's equality in both _____ and _____.

3.   The Risen Christ commissioned the first apostle—a _____.

4.   Euodia and Syntyche were _____ with Paul who worked with him, not under him.

5.   The _____ continued to advance the idea of equality of men and women in terms of substance and value, function and authority, privilege and responsibility.

6.   Tertullian who, in his early writings spoke vehemently against women, joined the _____ and modified his views, speaking respectfully of Maxmilla, Prisca, and a "gifted sister" in his congregation.

7.   _____, the official theologian of the Roman Catholic Church in the 13th century, believed that women "are defective and misbegotten" and totally inferior.

PART III   (Value: 7 items @ 2 each = 14 points)

Complete the sentences by selecting the best answers from the following list:

Hannah Whitall Smith ** Margaret Fell ** John Wesley ** Phoebe Palmer **
** Catherine Booth ** George Fox ** Katherine Bushnell **

1.   In 1666, _____ wrote Women Speaking Justified, the first major book written in favor of female public ministry.

2.   _____ considered Christ the only "Head."

3.   Regarding women in ministry, _____ said, "Who am I that I should withstand God?"

4.   Obedience to the call of God by _____ resulted her becoming the most influential leader of the Holiness Movement.

5.   _____, cofounder of the Salvation Army, was "an unfailing, unflinching, uncompromising champion of woman's rights" who staunchly refused to be considered or treated anything but equal with her husband.

6.   _____, a Quaker who wrote the classic book <u>The Christian's Secret of a Happy Life</u>, was deeply involved in movements with special concerns for the welfare and equality of women in society and in marriage.

7.   _____ wrote the classic book <u>God's Word to Women</u>.

PART IV	(Value: 10 items @ 2 each = 20 points)

Complete the sentences by selecting the best answers from the following list:

** authentein ** <u>teshuqa</u> ** archon ** <u>ezer</u> ** hupotasso **
** kephale ** ** egalitarian ** covering **

1.   The English word <u>helper</u> in Gen. 2:18, 20 is the Hebrew word derived from the root _____ meaning "to surround, protect, aid, help, succor" and it is used 14 times to refer to God and twice to refer to Eve.

2.   The word _____ in Gen. 3:16b, which has been traditionally translated "lust" or "desire" really means simply "turning." Thus the accurate meaning of this passage is that Eve is turning away from God to her husband, and God is warning her that this turning will result in her coming under the domination of her husband.

3.   _____ does not mean "head" in the sense of authority over or leadership, whereas the word _____ does carry this meaning, so if Paul had been talking about a man having authority over a woman, or one person having authority over another person, he would have chosen _____ rather than _____.

4.   Paul asks a married woman to identify with (_____), not come under the authority of her husband, as opposed to identifying with her birth family.

5.   Ephesians 5:15-18, accurately read, teaches mutual submission, that is, "submitting to one another," not the benevolent rulership of the man over the woman. This _____ way of life is based on "Be filled with the Spirit" (v. 18).

6.   _____ is a covenant word based on the idea of the Blood Covenant taking away sin; therefore, the idea of covering in the New Covenant refers to the Blood of Jesus erasing sin from the life of the believer. It has nothing to do with "authority over" or "accountability to."

7.   In 1 Tim. 2:12, Paul used the word_____. This is the only time this word is used in the New Testament, and Paul uses it in refuting ideas of female superiority coming from the cult of Artemis (Diana) in Ephesus.

APPENDIX 5

Answer Key to Examination

FINAL EXAM – ANSWER KEY

PART I		PART II		PART III		PART IV	
1.	True	1.	Jesus	1.	Margaret Fell	1.	ezer
2.	True	2.	marriage ministry	2.	George Fox	2.	teshuqa
3.	True	3.	woman	3.	John Wesley	3.	kephale archon archon kephale
4.	True	4.	coworkers	4.	Phoebe Palmer		
5.	True	5.	Spirit	5.	Catherine Booth	4.	hupotasso
6.	False	6.	Montanists	6.	Hannah Whitall Smith	5.	egalitarian
7.	True	7.	Aquinas	7.	Katherine Bushnell	6.	Covering
8.	False					7.	Authentein
9.	True						
10.	False						
11.	False						
12.	True						
13.	True						
14.	False						
15.	True						
16.	False						
17.	True						
18.	False						
19.	False						
20.	False						
21.	True						
22.	True						
23.	True						
24.	False						
25.	True						

Revival & Renewal Resources

HYATT PRESS
P. O. BOX 764463
DALLAS, TX 75376 USA

Drs. Eddie & Susan Hyatt are available to teach seminars and courses
related to their books and on other biblical and revival topics.

Also contact Eddie & Susan to help sponsor a conference in your area on
THE SPIRIT, THE BIBLE, & WOMEN

HyattPress@aol.com   Phone (214) 374-2454   Fax (214) 374-0252

TITLE	PRICE	QT	TOTAL
2000 YEARS OF CHARISMATIC CHRISTIANITY by Eddie L. Hyatt	$15.^{99}		
A HISTORY OF REVIVAL This teacher/student manual is designed to be used with the book *2000 Years of Charismatic Christianity*	$20.^{00}		
A HISTORY OF REVIVAL COURSE This includes the book *2000 Years of Charismatic Christianity* and the Manual.	$35.^{00}		
IN THE SPIRIT WE'RE EQUAL: The Spirit, The Bible, & Women—A Revival Perspective by Susan C. Hyatt	$16.^{99}		
THE SPIRIT, THE BIBLE, & WOMEN This teacher/student manual is designed to be used with the book *In the Spirit We're Equal.*	$20.^{00}		
THE SPIRIT, THE BIBLE, & WOMEN This includes the book *In the Spirit We're Equal* and the Manual.	$35.^{00}		
WHERE ARE MY SUSANNAS? by Susan C. Hyatt	$5.^{00}		
WONDERFUL WISDOM: A Study in Proverbs by Valarie Owen	$6.^{95}		
HEALING IN HIS WINGS: Scriptures for God's Healing by Valarie Owen	$5.^{95}		
FORGIVENESS: A COVENANT OF LOVE by Valarie Owen	$6.^{95}		
Coming Soon! **The MINISTRY OF THE HOLY SPIRIT**: A Bible Course and Teaching Manual on the Holy Spirit Eddie L. Hyatt	$15.^{00}		
Coming Soon! **WOMEN WHO LED THE WAY**: Women Who Founded the First Pentecostal Bible Schools by Susan C. Hyatt	$10.^{00}		
SUBTOTAL			
S/H in the US Add 10%			
TOTAL			

** Contact Hyatt Press for discounts on bulk orders. **
** These materials are also available in bookstores through Ingram/Spring Arbor. **

NAME _____
ADDRESS _____
E-MAIL OR PHONE _____